THI ꞮꞮꞮ

THE ISLANDS SERIES

---

* Published in the United States by Stackpole
All other titles published in the United States by David & Charles Inc
The series is distributed in Australia by Wren Publishing Pty Ltd, Melbourne

CORFU

by *BRIAN DICKS*

DAVID & CHARLES

NEWTON ABBOT LONDON NORTH POMFRET (VT) VANCOUVER

ISBN 0 7153 7311 0
Library of Congress Catalog Card Number
76–48823

© BRIAN DICKS 1977

Set in 11 on 13pt Monotype Baskerville
and printed in Great Britain
by Latimer Trend & Company Ltd Plymouth
for David & Charles (Publishers) Limited
Brunel House Newton Abbot Devon

Published in the United States of America
by David & Charles Inc
North Pomfret Vermont 05053 USA

Published in Canada
by Douglas David & Charles Limited
1875 Welch Street North Vancouver BC

CONTENTS

For my mother, who first saw me off to Greece

Fig 1 The I

and environs

1 CORFU IN CONTEXT

Somewhere between Calabria and Corfu the blue really begins. All the way across Italy you find yourself moving through a landscape severely domesticated – each valley laid out after the architects pattern, brilliantly lighted, human. But once you strike out from the flat and desolate Calabrian mainland towards the sea, you are aware of a change in the heart of things: aware of the horizon beginning to stain at the rim of the world: aware of *islands* coming out of the darkness to meet you.
Lawrence Durrell (*Prospero's Cell*)

THESE islands take the name Ionian from the sea in which they are situated – that section of the eastern Mediterranean basin lying south of the Strait of Otranto and between the foot of Italy and the Greek mainland (Fig 1). Strung along the western littoral of Greece, they have served throughout history as intermediaries between the Italian peninsula and the Levant, sharing in the civilisations, cultures and religions of both regions and providing a bridge over which armies and ideas moved. In antiquity the Ionian Islands lay between the city states of Greece and their 'colonial' settlements of Magna Graecia (southern Italy and Sicily), between Athens and Rome. During the medieval centuries they were situated on the borders between Western and Eastern Christendom and subsequently between Europe and the Moslem East. In the course of a long and colourful history the Ionian Islands have had many masters and witnessed wars, revolutions, sieges, naval battles, treacheries and power politics, yet out of this complicated background they have succeeded in establishing their own identity, not only as a group, but also individually.

In view of their peculiar 'Ionian stamp' the islands, Corfu in particular, have often been regarded as western anterooms to Greece, providing useful introductions to the country's landscape and way of life, although possessing atmospheres which ardent Philhellenes regard as un-Greek, or 'Greekish' – to use the adjective of the seventeenth-century traveller, Antony Shirley. In the physical sense, especially to the visitor approaching Greece from Italy, the Ionian Islands convey a delusive impression of the country's fertility for they receive the highest rainfall of all Greek lands and consequently even in summer their vegetation cover is luxuriant. On the human level, however, critics of the non-Hellenic character of the islands are apt to be misled, for in spite of their remnants and undertones of foreign influence the Ionian Islands are and always have been undeniably Greek. The Greek language has remained the common tongue throughout the centuries and the peasant classes maintained their traditional way of life with the innate conservatism of all Mediterranean peoples. The Orthodox Church, the other great bastion of Greek life, provided further cultural continuity and in spite of some Latinised trappings there is no doctrinal differences between the Ionian Church and the Church of Greece with which it was united in the nineteenth century.

The name Ionian is misleading and would seem to be a more appropriate term for the eastern Aegean islands of Samos, Chios and Lesbos which in antiquity lay off the Asia Minor coast of Greek Ionia; but there is no truth in the theory that the islands were settled by ancient Ionian colonists. Scholars have pointed out that Ionia and the Ionians take their name from their founder hero Ion, whereas the Ionian Sea is called after the nymph, or goddess, Io. According to Aeschylus the love-affair between Zeus and the beautiful Io had angered Hera who spied on the guilty couple through an eye in a peacock's tail. To allay Hera's suspicions the willing maiden was changed by her divine lover into a heifer. Zeus was above punishment and reproach so Hera ordered a gadfly to sting the cow which, maddened by pain, plunged into the sea. After a marathon swim Io reached Egypt and was restored to human form to become the first of a long line of beauties particularly pleasing to the gods. Thus from at least the sixth century BC there are references to the Ionian Sea or Gulf, but it is interesting that the title 'Ionian Islands' is a conception of nineteenth-century politics. In 1800, for example, it was used by the Russian Admiral Ousakov in a proclamation to the inhabitants of what the Venetians had known as the 'Isole di Levante'.

In the conventional use of the term the Ionian Islands include the larger entities of Corfu, Paxos, Lefkas, Ithaca, Cefalonia, Zakinthos (Zante) and Cythera, and are also known as the *Heptanesus* – the 'Seven Islands'. Cythera, although belonging traditionally to the group, is situated in a southerly position off the eastern peninsula of the Peloponnesus and has largely shared the fate of southern Greece. In addition to the seven main islands there are numerous smaller ones, some attractive and fertile like Antipaxos, others no more than uninhabited rocks. The entire group nominally forms one of Greece's nine administrative regions with its capital at Corfu. The region is further divided into departments or *nomoi* based on Corfu, Lefkas, Cefalonia and Zakinthos. The islands of Paxos and Antipaxos, together with the small Othonian or Thiapondi islands of Fanos, Merlera and Mathraki to the north-west, belong to the *nomos* of Corfu.

The name 'Corfu' appears to be a corruption of the Byzantine Greek *korufai* (breasts), referring to the fortified twin rocks where the population took refuge in times of siege and which became the nucleus of the medieval town. In antiquity, however, the island was known by a variety of names, many of these titles highly descriptive but ephemeral. Homer and other writers refer to Corfu as *Shetia* or *Scheria*, the traditional homeland of the *Odyssey*'s Phaecaeans who were ruled by Alcinous and his daughter Nausicaa. A legendary account tells how the island was threatened with being joined to the mainland by the infilling of the Corfu Channel with deposits from the Epirot rivers. Demeter, goddess of earth and agriculture, and protectress of the island, appealed to Poseidon for help and the island became known as *Scheria*, meaning 'to hold back'. Less romantically the name *Scheria* is said to derive from the Phoenician word *scara*, meaning commerce.

Corfu's other early names include *Drepanum* and *Kerkyra*. The former comes from the Greek word for a scythe or cutting hook and refers to the island's peculiar shape. Another legend claims that each evening, before retiring to Mount Olympus, Demeter concealed her scythe under Corfu and gradually the island moulded itself to the shape of the tool, eventually taking its name. It requires a certain amount of imagination to reconstruct the form of the scythe but Corfu extends north to south as a great crescent for over 6okm and its width varies from 4km to a maximum of 20. The 'handle' of the scythe lies in the region of Chlomos and Lefkimi in the south and the great sweep of the cutting edge (north to Mount Pandocrator), is interrupted only by the promontories in the vicinity of Corfu town.

Kerkyra (Latin Corcyra) was Corfu's most widely used name in antiquity. It is first given by Corinthian colonists and Diodorus links it with the name of a legendary hero. More probably, however, it is derived from words such as *korfos* (gulf), or *kerkouros* (a fish), or *kerikos* (a tail, handle), the latter perhaps again stressing the peculiarity of the island's configuration. Other scholarship has related the name to the Phoenician word *carcara* (abundance) or to an Illyrian version of a native Greek name which also occurs in Korcyra Nigra in the Adriatic. N. G. L. Hammond is of the opinion that *Kerkyra* is related in some way to the modern Albanian word *kyark*, meaning a curve. Whatever the derivation it is interesting that the island's modern Greek name has preserved the ancient Corinthian appellation and in keeping with the major part of insular Greece, both island and its capital carry the same form of *i Kerkyra* – a feminine noun.

Corfu is not the largest of the Ionian Islands (580 sq km compared with Cefalonia's 737 sq km), but economically it is the most important and has the largest population – 99,092 inhabitants of which 29,896 reside in Corfu town. The island's geographical position at the entrance to the Adriatic has given it greater strategic significance than its southern neighbours for it is both the nearest Greek territory to Italy (74km distant) and its northern cape, Varvara, is less than 3km from the coast of Albania from which it is separated by the Corfu Channel. The Greek–Albanian frontier reaches the coastal range south-east of Konispol, but follows the crest north-eastwards to Cape Stilo, reserving the southern slopes to Greece. This international boundary, however, has been hotly contested by Greece and Albania during this century.

Corfu's history vividly reveals the conditioning influence of this geographical position which has meant that insularity has proved the very antithesis of isolation. It has been the chief determinant in the island's chequerboard development which, although variable in detail, has a stubborn sameness in its general pattern. Corfu has been the battleground of contending cultures and of conflicting political and commercial interests, for strategists and statesmen of both East and West regarded the island as a possession of great value. In antiquity Corinthians, Athenians, Spartans, Syracusans, Illyrians and Romans represent some of the rival powers bent on securing the island and the entrance to the Adriatic. Throughout the medieval centuries it was the political pawn in the ideological game between Western Europe and the Byzantine empire and Corfu's significance as a naval and commercial base is emphasised by its subsequent affiliation to Venice, a domination which lasted for 400 years. By the end of the eighteenth century France, the Ottoman Empire, Russia and Britain looked on Corfu with envy for it became part of the expansionist plans of all these nations. Bonaparte viewed the island as a springboard to the East and Britain saw its possession as a major factor in the 'Eastern Question'. In 1864, following centuries of foreign rule, Corfu and the Ionian Islands were united with Greece, but their value as vital strategic bases was again evident during

World War I, the Balkan Wars and World War II, substantiating British nineteenth-century military opinion that the 'power with influence in the Ionian Islands would eventually determine the fate of Greece'.

As an integral part of the Greek state, modern Corfu continues to draw people of all lands to its shores. They come not as conquerors, but as visitors or settlers and their numbers increase annually. Since the late fifties the island has benefited considerably from investment in tourism and Corfu is not only pre-eminent as a holiday centre among the Ionian Islands, but also ranks as one of the main resorts of Greece. Many are attracted solely by the island's climate, beaches and modern hotel complexes, but others seek their interests in the tangible remains of Corfu's earlier civilisations and in an atmosphere which recalls the 'times past' of Europe. To many people, Britons in particular, Corfu has become the ideal place for permanent residence. For them the island's traditional role is reversed for Corfu, the conquered island of history, is today the conqueror.

Plate 1 The old Venetian fort and the southern section of the Esplanade. The rotunda is Corfu's memorial to Sir Thomas Maitland

Plate 2 A roof-top view of part of the highly congested old town of Corfu

Plate 3   The coast near Benitses, looking north

Plate 4   The Vlachernai Monastery and Mouse Island viewed from Kanoni – Corfu's famous beauty spot

2   GARDEN OF THE IONIAN

'CORFU is an enchanting island, soft and green, lying in the blue Ionian Sea off Epirus. Thickly covered with olive trees and cypresses, fringed with sandy beaches and shingle coves, with its rocky mountains soaring straight from the sea to the north, all combine to make it a delight for the traveller.' This lucid description is typical of official guidebooks and brochures designed by tour-operators to sell package holidays in what is now one of Greece's major vacation regions. It is not much of an exaggeration. The beauty and fertility of Corfu have long been famous and not without justification has it been called an 'earthly paradise', the 'Venus of the isles' and the 'garden of the Ionian'. The nineteenth century in particular provided many writers and artists who through prose, verse and canvas attempted to capture the island's atmosphere, but none more successfully than Edward Lear. In 1858 he wrote: 'This place is wonderfully lovely. I wish you could see it; if you come I could put you up beautifully on ginger-beer, and claret, and prawns, and figs.' His *Views in the Seven Ionian Islands* is a work that accurately reflects the quality of the Corfiote landscape more than any other.

Poetic fancy aside, the attractiveness of the Corfiote landscape is founded firmly on prosaic fact. The island's physical form is the result of an eventful geological and erosional history and its environment is enhanced by a climate which is the embodiment of a number of peculiar meteorological conditions. The resultant vegetation cover, with its profusion and rich variety of species, adds further dimensions to Corfu's composite natural beauty, whereas on the human level its cosmo-

B

politan flavour is the happy result of centuries of unbroken civilisation.

STRUCTURE AND TOPOGRAPHY

Corfu and the other Ionian Islands are detached portions of the belt of high fold mountains that extend throughout the western Balkans from the Dinaric Alps in Bosnia, through Montenegro and Albania, to become the Pindus system of mainland Greece and its extension southwards into the Peloponnesus. The folding was contemporaneous with the great Alpine earth-movements of Tertiary times and was succeeded by considerable vertical faulting often transverse to the main north-west to south-east structural trends. The physical separation of the islands and the indented form of their coastlines is related to east–west fracture zones parallel to those responsible for the Gulfs of Patras and Corinth which separate the Peloponnesus from mainland Greece. Structural adjustments along these lines of weakness have continued to the present, and major zones of seismic activity are associated with the islands of Zakinthos, Lefkas and Cefalonia. Although not immune to earthquakes, Corfu was untouched by the devastating tremors that destroyed the town of Zakinthos in 1953. Cefalonia has also been reduced to ruin and the town of Lefkas was destroyed in 1878 and again in 1948.

The geological and physiographic structure of Corfu is related to the fold mountains of Greek Epirus and Albania. These mainland regions consist of a number of hill and lofty mountain-ranges with broad intervening longitudinal valleys trending from north-west to south-east in alignment with the Adriatic shore. The rocks are of Mesozoic and Tertiary age and, generally speaking, Jurassic–Cretaceous limestones are succeeded to the east by progressively younger formations – although folding and faulting has led to a complicated repetition of this pattern. The presence of massive limestone formations, visible in anticlines, is responsible for the major relief features and, being permeable, has resulted in irregular erosional forms.

The term *karst* is applied to limestone country that is partly or wholly without surface drainage; and sink holes (*katavothra*), underground streams and associated erosional features are characteristic of many localities. Surrounding the limestones are deposits of Oligocene–Eocene and Pliocene–Miocene age which consist of varieties of sandstone, marl, clay and conglomerate. Known to Alpine geologists as *flysch*, or 'the sediments that slip', they are for the most part impermeable and streams are numerous during the rainy season. Being less-resistant formations, the *flysch* zones are subject to extensive erosion by autumnal and winter rains, especially where deforestation has taken place and the result is a characteristic 'bad-land' topography of barren surfaces with numerous deep and irregular gullies. Recent structural disturbances have also produced more resistant conglomerates and quartzites – metamorphic rocks formed as the result of pressure and high temperature on the folded sedimentary cover.

This parallel arrangement of rock outcrops and relief features is less marked in Corfu than in mainland localities, but the geological structure of the island is clearly reflected in its topography (Figs 2 and 3). The general form of Corfu is conditioned by Jurassic and Cretaceous limestones although these are not exposed so extensively, nor elevated so considerably, as in Epirus or in the islands to the south. The principal area of limestone is confined to the north where a mountainous block, also containing many siliceous beds, extends from Capes Varvara and Kassiopis on the east coast to Cape Falakron on the west. The highest altitude is reached in the Pandocrator massif (906m) where the limestone deposits are particularly thick, and other significant heights include Stravroskiadi (850m) and Lasi (830m). Large sections of this upland gives rise to rugged topography with stretches of high waterless tablelands with karstic features and deeply ravined slopes. West of Pandocrator the limestone belt contracts, summits are lower (Tsouka 631m and Arakli 510m), and at its seaward termination there are imposing cliffs at Palaeokastritsa on the northern

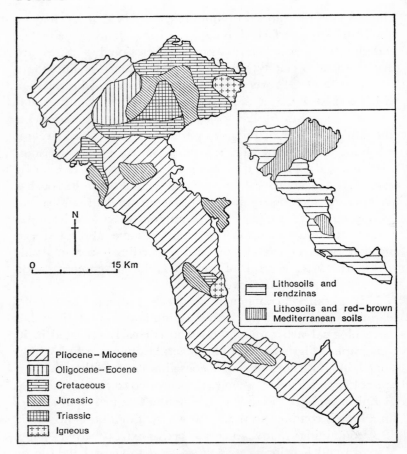

Fig 2   Solid geology and generalised soil types

side of Liapades Bay. The limestone-based soils are thin and
infertile and belong to the generalised classifications of lithosoils
and red-brown Mediterranean soils. Although termed 'soils',
the former show little soil development and form a thin cover
over bedrock and are agriculturally unproductive. Red-brown
Mediterranean soils occur in small scattered basins and develop
after the soluble constituents of the limestone have been re-

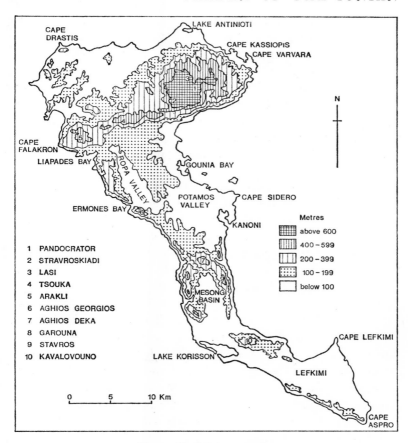

Fig 3   Corfu's topography

moved. Their calcium and organic content is low and they have a neutral or alkaline reaction.

To the north and west of the uplands altitude falls to produce a triangular area of land developed on Tertiary sands, clays and marls, bordered by alluvial and swampy coasts. This variety of deposits provides a detailed and confused topography of irregularly eroded basins and a maze of low hills deeply cut by stream courses. Regions such as this, as the density of rural

23

settlement shows, are of great economic importance to the island for their fertile and water-retaining soils form the basis of Corfiote agriculture and they often carry woodland and pasture. In the valleys and along the coasts there are wide stretches of alluvium which when reclaimed provide fertile soils for agriculture. The region is drained by the Fonissa and lesser streams but owing to the summer drought there are few permanent water-courses. However, springs and wells in these Tertiary formations provide sufficient water to maintain cultivation.

South of the limestone uplands the island narrows abruptly and forms an eastward-facing basin which is structurally continued into Albania and Epirus. The west coast, broken by Ermones Bay, is bounded by a steep south-easterly trending ridge which rises to 392m in Aghios Georgios. This is a continuation of the northern uplands and to the east it is flanked by Livadi Ropa, a lowland 10km long and 1 to 3km wide, developed to Tertiary sediments. Owing on its gentle fall to the south it was formerly swampy and subject to extensive winter flooding. 'The angel of death hovers over this wide plain,' wrote Anstead in 1863, 'death in the terrible form of a wasting and poisonous fever. Here are always at hand the seeds of malaria ready to attack every victim who comes within their influence.' The valley is drained through a gorge in the coastal ridge to Ermones Bay and, now reclaimed (see Chapter 10), it forms a rich agricultural area.

The Ropa valley is separated from the Tertiary lowlands of the east coast by a conglomerate outcrop which marks the watershed of east- and west-flowing drainage. The eastern lowlands of Pliocene sands and clays consist of a number of small basins, some with interior drainage, but the most important river is the north-flowing Potamos which reaches the sea to the north of Corfu town. The coast is low and marshy, but is broken by a number of small bays bordered in places by mud-banks. To the south of Cape Kommeno is Gounia harbour entered by a narrow channel through mud-banks. In the neighbourhood of Corfu town the coastline is higher and the town itself stands on a rocky promontory which terminates in Cape Sidero. To the south is the shallow Garitsa Bay followed by the narrow Kanoni peninsula which encloses Lake Chalikiopoulos to the west.

Jurassic and Cretaceous limestones reappear in the Aghios Deka range (576m) which separates the central area of the island from its narrow southern section. Two highland branches extend from it along the western and eastern coasts – Garouna (466m) and Stavros (427m) respectively – and both descend steeply to the sea. They enclose the Mesongi basin, an area filled with Pliocene sands and gravels, but broken by hills of more resistant conglomerates. Southwards, Corfu's lower elevation is broken only by Kavalovouno (330m), although the western coast is hillier and more abrupt than the eastern with the hills of the former continuing to Cape Aspro, the south-eastern extremity of the island. Other characteristics of the south are areas of swamp where impervious layers of clay occur, and a number of coastal salt-water lagoons. The largest, Limni (Lake) Korisson, extends for nearly 5km along the west coast and is separated from the sea by a narrow sand spit. In the nineteenth century this too was the source of malaria which made its neighbourhood uninhabitable. In the south-east a triangular area of land containing a lagoon and salt pans runs out to Cape Lefkimi. Both the marshes and the lagoons are rich in plant and wildlife.

CLIMATE

'Climate' is an abstraction thought up by geographers, and climatic generalisations, although necessary to classification, are rarely satisfactory in describing local situations, especially when referring to an area the size of Corfu. The Mediterranean type of climate experienced on the southern Adriatic coast is often summed up in the words 'warm wet winters and hot dry summers' and this description must be considerably modified before anything like the true picture of the conditions prevailing

25

on the island emerges. Whereas Corfu follows the general Mediterranean seasonal pattern, its climate differs appreciably from other parts of 'Mediterranean' Greece. This is the result of a variety of local factors in the form of topography, aspect, nearness to the sea and to continental masses. Contrasts occur not only between the island and the adjacent mainland but also with other insular areas where a similar parallel might be expected. The major difference is associated with Corfu's average rainfall which, although confined largely to the winter months (Fig 4), is heavier and of longer duration than that common for much of Greece. This is reflected in a vegetation cover which even in summer appears green and luxuriant, offering a bold contrast to the barren and parched hillsides of mainland Greece and the Aegean.

Corfu's rainfall is chiefly associated with the passage of

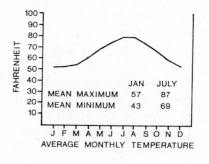

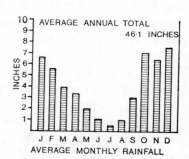

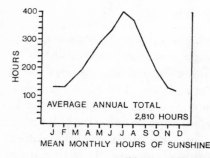

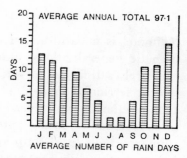

Fig 4   Climatological graphs

depressions eastwards across the Mediterranean basin, some originating in the Atlantic, others within the Mediterranean area. The deep land-locked trough of the Adriatic has a low-pressure area of its own and once established by the upward currents of warm air, frequent depressions move in the same direction as other Mediterranean cyclones. These depressions impinge on the upland areas of Albania and Epirus causing heavy rainfall between October and March. Although generally absent during the summer months, particularly June, July and August, rain can occur in the form of violent thunder and hail-storms which temper the heat but are often disastrous to harvests and soil cover. Thunderstorms also occur in late September when the pattern is one of short heavy downpours interspersed with bright sunny periods. Only in December is rainfall consistently heavy when Corfu has been likened to a sub-tropical Ireland. The sharp seasonal differences are reflected in the discharge of streams. In winter they are broad deep torrents, often causing serious flooding to lowland areas, while in summer they dry up or their braided channels trickle through extensive sheets of flood gravel.

The climatological data (Fig 4), based on readings taken over thirty years in Corfu, Zakinthos and Argostoli, summarise the island's seasonal pattern. As the means suggest temperatures can soar into the nineties (fahrenheit) in July and August and can fall below freezing-point in January and February. The latter conditions, however, are not common, and the January average is 50° F making frost a rarity (although not unknown) and confining snow to the summits of the principal hills. In general terms the summer heat is not as intense as in Athens but excessive humidity often makes it less tolerable. The summer months were often a severe trial to the British troops stationed in Corfu during the first half of the nineteenth century, but conditions are alleviated by frequent sea breezes. Summer temperatures persist far into autumn. This is a maritime feature related to the retention of summer heat by sea-water. Corfu's most temperate periods are spring and late autumn, the former characterised by a profusion of wild flowers and the latter by cooler sunny days and the occasional rainstorm.

One of the principal features of Corfu's climate is its liability to sudden change. This is a function of both the frequency of diurnal breezes, caused by the unequal heating of land and sea, and to the stronger seasonal winds which originate within and beyond the Mediterranean basin. Unlike the Aegean, the Ionian Sea is less affected by the northerly *meltemi* – the summer 'trade-wind' that sweeps across south-eastern Greece with particular vehemence. The prevailing wind in winter is from the south-east and in summer from the north-west – the *maestros*. In some years, especially in June and August, Corfu is affected by the *sirokos*, a sticky south-westerly wind which originates over North Africa. This is not so virulent on the west coast of Greece as in Malta and Sicily, but when it blows it leaves the population short-tempered and fretful. It lasts for very short periods but for Private Wheeler in a letter dated 'Corfu, July 20, 1823', it was 'the disagreablest evil' with which he had to contend.

FLORA AND FAUNA

To the visitor arriving by ship, Corfu announces itself by the heavy scent of pines, herbs and citrus groves. Travelling within it the scenery has been likened to the greenness of the English countryside, although in Corfu it is combined with the characteristic Greek seascape. 'Venus in her beard green' is Simpson's (*Greece – The Unclouded Eye*) poetic description of the island's lushness which is not solely related to its high rainfall totals. The fact that Corfu escaped Ottoman domination was also beneficial to the vegetation cover. In other parts of Greece the Turks neglected agriculture and afforestation, contributing little more than a proliferation of the ubiquitous goat whose affect on vegetation cover was disastrous. In contrast, the Venetians encouraged and rewarded the planting of trees, especially the olive which today contributes greatly to Corfu's income. The cypress, often growing alongside the olive, is another characteristic of the island's scenery.

But Corfu has not escaped the ravages of soil erosion, fire and over-grazing, and the destruction of the vegetation cover has been progressive. Much of the original forest cover has either been removed or modified by man and, as elsewhere in Greece and the Mediterranean basin, this has been replaced by a low-order scrub community known as *maquis*. It results from secondary colonisation of former forestland or of land passing out of cultivation, and consists of thickets of shrubs, sometimes as high as 2m. Myrtle, tree heather, holm oak and Aleppo pine are found in what is defined as 'high' *maquis* and often develop into proper woodlands. In 'low' *maquis* trees are rare and are replaced by a tangled growth of aromatic bushes, none of which grow above a metre. A further stage of degeneration is reached in the *garigue*, although this is not as common in Corfu as in parts of mainland Greece and the Aegean. The term is applied to stony dried-out ground with small scattered bushes, many of them again aromatic – lavender, rosemary, thyme, sage, garlic and rue.

In spring the scrub communities burst into flower for a wide variety of bulbous and tuberous plants are associated with them – the wild ancestors of the tulip, iris, crocus and hyacinth. The flowering period rises to its peak at the end of April and a striking feature is the mass effect of certain flowers both on hillsides and in fields. At different times different areas are carpeted with masses of one plant – shepherd's purse, buttercup, speedwell, field marigold, wild geranium, corn marigold and chamomile. The spring blaze of meadow colour is short-lived but there are few periods when wild flowers are not in bloom and during the summer months there are varieties of thistles together with rockroses, scabious, clematis and bellflowers. Temperatures are such that some plants continue to grow throughout the winter and many species are revived with the September rains.

The park-like character of much of the island is provided by clumps of deciduous oak, silver poplar and eucalyptus trees. Other common varieties are the cypress, the plane, a number of pines and above all the olive which untended attains the size and dignity of a forest tree. Cultivated trees include varieties of citrus, and almost every village has apple, pear, cherry, peach, apricot, fig, mulberry, almond and walnut. Many of the trees and shrubs of Corfu town are unknown or rare in Britain. They include the Judas tree, California pepper tree, jacaranda, Indian bead tree, loquat, agave, prickly pear and a number of palms. The majority are not indigenous to the island but are now naturalised in their Mediterranean environment.

The construction of roads and hotel complexes and the re-placement of natural vegetation by cultivated species has driven many animals from their native haunts, yet the wide range of wildlife complements Corfu's rich array of plant communities. Most numerous and varied are the birds which include wagtails, sparrows, goldfinches, chaffinches, greenfinches, larks, magpies and crows. There are also owls, of which the white barn-owl is a rare specimen, together with woopoes, jays and kingfishers. Herons and other waders are found at lakes Korisson and Lefkimi and there are birds of prey such as kestrels, buzzards and eagles. Corfu has a number of species of seagull and spring brings the cuckoo, the swallow and the house martin.

The island is one of the few places in Europe where jackals are found and other wild mammals are foxes, hares, bats, weasels, hedgehogs, and small rodents. In spring tortoises are seen in the undergrowth and frogs and terrapins are found in perennial pools. There is some confusion over the numbers and types of snake, but there are two varieties of viper, one like the British adder and the other, equally venomous, is more brightly coloured. Other snakes are harmless and there are many lizards. Among the insects the cicadas and fireflies are the most obvious, the latter especially in mid-May when they herald the approach of summer. Corfu also has scorpions although these are rarely seen.

3   MYTHS, HEROES AND HISTORY

FROM legend to history is a short step in the Ionian Islands. The two are so interwoven that scholars have either despaired in attempting to decipher fact from fiction, or else have forwarded some lively views and theories, some more plausible than others, to explain the geographical mysteries of Greek folk memory. Homer in the *Odyssey* has left a fascinating if tantalising description of Scheria, the land of the Phaecaeans and the scene of the shipwrecked Odysseus' romantic episode with Nausicaa, the beautiful and determined daughter of King Alcinous. Since antiquity the island of Corfu has been equated with Scheria and it has been the aspiration of archaeologists, and of *Odyssey* lovers the world over, to trace the site of Alcinous' noble city which Homer stated stood on a headland between two harbours. A number of sites have contended for the situation of the palace with its 'bronze walls and golden doors hung on posts of silver'. For many years the chosen spot was the Palaeopolis or Kanoni peninsula south of Corfu town, lying between the Chalikiopoulos lagoon and Garitsa Bay. The off-shore island of Pondikonisi (Mouse Island) traditionally represents the petrified ship of Odysseus. Homer's account, however, describes a high mountain above the Scherian capital for Poseidon, not content with wrecking Odysseus' ship, attempted to cut the island off from the rest of the world. Archaeologists such as Bérard and Dorpfeld also turned their attention to the northern and western coasts, scanning the creeks, headlands and cliffs for physical details that fitted Homer's description.

In 1901, Victor Bérard, on topographical rather than

archaeological grounds, concentrated his research on Palaeokastritsa in the north-west and decided that this was the most
likely site for the ancient settlement, for a high mountain-range
sweeps down to a coast fretted with small bays and headlands
(Fig 5). He placed the king's palace on the promontory now
dominated by the present monastery of the Virgin Mary which
dates from the thirteenth century. The twin ports of the
Phaecaeans he equated with the trefoil-shaped bay, Port Alipa,
and Port St Spyridon. Bérard regarded the agora as occupying
the intervening isthmus. He suggested that the vineyards and
olive groves of Alcinous occupied the terraced ground at the
foot of the mountain and the petrified ship was the islet of
Vigla, which lay to the south in view of the harbours. This site
corresponds with the details given by Homer and the coast

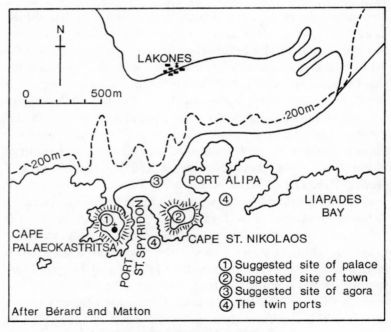

Fig 5   The Palaeokastritsa Region

would certainly have been the one approached by a raft or small boat from the west when Odysseus arrived from the island home of Circe. Unfortunately no single archaeological find has substantiated this fanciful theory. Other archaeologists, including Dorpfeld, explored similar sites on the north coast such as Aphiona and Kassiopi, all with the necessary topographical criteria presented by Homer, but the material evidence, plentiful in the form of earthenware objects, in no way matched the *Odyssey*'s description of a rich and culturally advanced palacecity. Since the early years of this century, scholars, discouraged by inconclusive or negative results, have largely abandoned the *Odyssey* quest and Homer the poet has once again replaced Homer the historian. But indifferent to the researchers and statements of scholars, the *Odyssey* legend lives on in Corfu and it is doubtful whether the land of the Phaecaeans will ever be displaced from the popular folklore of the island, probably because myths always appear more attractive than reality. 'Across the rich screen of this island,' writes Lawrence Durrell, 'many names, ancient and modern, offer themselves to the mind like the translation of flesh into ghostly appearances which still delude the living by their resemblance to them.'

THE ARCHAEOLOGICAL EVIDENCE

Apart from the rich legacy of myths, folklore, epic sagas and genealogical histories, knowledge of Corfu in the prehistoric period, down to the appearance of proto-Corinthian remains at Palaeopolis in the late eighth century BC, is based almost entirely on the excavations of H. Bulle at Aphiona on the northwest coast. New metal-working techniques from the east had spread to the southern islands of Cefalonia, Ithaca, Lefkas and Zakinthos after 3000 BC, but Corfu continued to evolve its own sub-Neolithic culture – a protracted development which continued well into the Greek Bronze Age. It appears from the evidence of pottery and other archaeological discoveries that a significant cultural divide existed in the Ionian Sea to the north and south of Lefkas. The southern islands, Cefalonia in particular, formed the centres of a flourishing civilisation similar to Peloponnesian Mycenae in the fifteenth century BC. Mycenaean tombs, common to Cefalonia, Zakinthos and also Lefkas, have not been found on Corfu.

Explanations for Corfu's retarded development are numerous. According to a tradition preserved by the ancient topographer Strabo, the island was inhabited by Illyrian tribes from the Adriatic coasts and this view is strengthened by prehistoric remains analogous to those of Apulia on the Italian mainland. Corfu may well have been more vigorously connected with the west than with the main centres of Greek progress and the occupation of the island by less-advanced and probably warlike peoples deterred its colonisation by Mycenaean settlers and traders.

The Aphiona peninsula – one of the suggested sites for the Phaecaean capital – is linked to the main part of the island by a narrow spit. On the peninsula an easily defended hill called Nisos and an area of more level ground, called Katzenfeld by Bulle, have revealed pottery styles that belong to different periods. The fine ware from Nisos, with incised decorations and cord impressions, is related both to the unpainted Neolithic wares of Motfetta, near Bari in southern Italy, and to sites in the Nidhri plain of Lefkas. They date from the Late Neolithic and Early Bronze Age periods. The Katzenfeld yielded a coarser ware, similar in every respect to sites in Epirus, but again to sites in the Nidhri plain. Bulle concluded that the Aphiona sites were separate in time with Katzenfeld belonging to a later date. Nisos appears to have been occupied to defend the peninsula from the main part of the island and Katzenfeld was settled when defence was no longer important, presumably when the island was occupied by similar or related peoples. In excavations at Cape Kefali a few miles north of Aphiona, Dorpfeld reported a similar culture to that of the Nidhri plain where pottery was coarse and monochrome and only a few sherds showed the characteristic Mycenaean styles and glazings.

Plate 5 (right) The rugged north-west coast at Palaeokastritsa

Plate 6 (below) The Venetian-built canal separates the Old Fort from the Esplanade

Contrasting architecture:
Plate 7 (left) The twelfth-century
Byzantine church of St Jason and
St Sosipatros at Anemomilos
Plate 8 (below) The neo-classical
façade of the Palace of St Michael
and St George

The conclusions to Corfu's prehistoric cultures remain hazy and problematic, but Sordinas reports that this primitive pottery has deep roots in Epirus; that it extended in time to beyond the Mycenaean period; and that it appeared in Apulia at an early date. Further excavations may well reveal Mycenaean artefacts, but it seems doubtful that these will be of sufficient importance to place Corfu within the sphere of Mycenaean political and economic influence. The island's prehistoric peoples were conversant with seamanship, as the choice of the Aphiona and Cape Kefali settlements show, and these were probably sporadic ports of call for Mycenaean ships, thus explaining the limited distribution of their wares.

A COLONY OF CORINTH

From the mists and myths of time emerges the first historical date, for in 734 BC the city of Corcyra was founded as a 'colonial' settlement of Corinth. Its site was the Palaeopolis or Kanoni peninsula a little to the south of modern Corfu town. Colonisation was a regular activity in pre-classical and classical times and the exploration of the West by peoples of the Greek mainland and Aegean brought the Ionian Islands into the political and economic orbits of the city states. Greek colonisation was seaborne and the reasons behind it included the expansion of trading connections, land hunger and over-population in the longer-settled areas of eastern Greece. The colonies were planted on islands or on coastal sites, often at the expense of native peoples, and when the colonies themselves expanded, they too developed further settlements on similar sites. Rarely did the colonists venture into the hinterland for their success was dependent on seamanship. In every respect the Greek colony was 'a settlement far from home' (*apoikia*) and the new state became a replica of the old. The colonists set out under a leader (*oikistes*) and took with them the religious and political institutions of their mother-city – cults, dialect, constitution and calendar etc. But once the colony was securely established

c

the cord with the founder city was cut and although strong emotional ties often continued, the new settlement acquired complete political independence. There are only a few examples of founder cities claiming political rights over colonies. Corinth, for example, which had founded a large colonial empire, demanded precedence in joint ceremonies with its offsprings and often sent magistrates and other officials to check on internal affairs.

The site for Corcyra was chosen less with the view of further exploitation of the seas to the north than as a port of call on the trading routes to the west. The Corfu Channel offered shelter from the strongest westerlies and was therefore a useful waiting-place for shipping making the crossing to Sicily and Italy with their numerous Greek colonies. The native inhabitants at this time remain a mystery for in addition to the Phaecaeans the early writers also refer to Colchians, Eretrians and Liburnians, many of whom were expelled by the Corinthians. The presence of Colchians is particularly suspect for they stem from Argonaut traditions and the account of their settlement on Corfu was greatly embroidered by Apollonius Rhodius who relied chiefly on folklore for his authority.

There are firmer grounds for accepting Eretrian settlement. The earliest colonists of Italy and Sicily came from the Euboean cities of Chalcis and Eretria and it appears that on route to the West they planted a colony at Corcyra with possessions on the Epirot mainland. The presence of Euboeans at Corcyra is implied by their emblem (a cow suckling a calf) on Corcyraean coins. It is also significant that the peninsula on which the Corinthian colony stood was known as Macridie, a Euboean name, and that there was a place Euboea on the island.

Strabo is the chief source for the Liburnians and his statements have been variously interpreted. One view supports them as being the native peoples prior to Eretrian colonisation, and another that they were a seafaring people who controlled part of the island and were therefore potential rivals of the Corinthians – hence their expulsion.

The manner in which the native peoples were treated by

Corinth remains uncertain, but in view of the rapid economic and political expansion of the colony in the Greek world it seems probable that Corcyra incorporated many of the earlier inhabitants into the state and so had a large free population. The city's rise to power in such a short time could not have taken place had it remained an exclusively Corinthian settlement. Strabo uses a term meaning 'joint settlement' when talking of the foundation of Corcyra and N. G. L. Hammond considers that this was with Greek-speaking natives for there is no indication of non-Hellenic terms in the Corcyraean dialect.

RICHES AND REVOLT

The colony planted at Corcyra, the first and the largest of several (Fig 6), was the means by which Corinth consciously sought a permanent trading position in the West. Others were founded at Molycrium, Macynia, Chalcis and Oeniadae, all controlling the entrance to the Gulf of Corinth and to these were added colonies at Lefkas and Ambracia. Jointly with Corcyra a colony was founded at Anactorium near the mouth of the Gulf of Ambracia, but the active exploration of the Adriatic coasts was largely the initiative of Corcyra itself. The Euboeans had founded settlements on the Epirot coast and at Oricum to the north, on the borders of Illyria. Of these cities only stray references are made by the ancient authors. Of considerable significance to the future relationships between Corcyra and Corinth was the colony of Epidamnus (Roman Dyrrhachium, modern Durazzo). This was founded by Corcyra in 627 BC and was located 240km to the north on the Adriatic coast. It was followed around 600 BC by Apollonia, another mixed Greek and Illyrian settlement attributed to both Corcyra and Corinth. A further move along the Adriatic coast was also sponsored by Corcyra who aided the Cnidians of the eastern Aegean to settle Corcyra Nigra (Korčula), an island in the Dalmatian Archipelago. From these positions of strategic importance Corinth and its colonies controlled the export of

39

Fig 6 Western Greece in Antiquity

silver, pastoral products and ship-timber, and the distribution of early Corinthian coinage illustrates the geographical extent of the city's trading influence. Coins based on the Corcyraean variant of the Corinthian standard have been found in various parts of the Adriatic, including the eastern Etruscan cities of

40

the Italian peninsula. Corinth was undoubtedly the greatest centre of exchange in the Mediterranean area, but the separate coinage of Corcyra is the first mark of the island's emancipation from Corinthian control.

Both Thucydides and Herodotus speak of the hostility and long-standing competitive jealousy which seems to have existed between Corcyra and Corinth since the foundation of the colony. The root cause was the island's geographical advantages for it quickly accumulated wealth and power and, arrogant by the possession of a strong navy, it was able to break the links with Corinth. The Corinthians retaliated in what is reputed to be the first recorded naval battle in history. It took place in the straits of Corfu in 665 BC when the navy of Corinth was defeated and the island established its political independence. Subsequently the island was brought to heel and Herodotus recounts how Periander of Corinth (c 625–586 BC), as a savage reprisal, sent 300 youths from leading Corcyraean families to be castrated at Lydia. The ships put in at Samos and aided by the Samians the youths escaped. Following the downfall of the Corinthian tyranny in 582 BC, Corcyra again became independent and the majority of the island's archaeological remains, which testify to the city's wealth and culture, belong to this period. The variety of Corcyra's trading contacts is shown by pottery at Palaeopolis of proto-Corinthian, Attic, Laconian and Rhodian or Milesian wares.

THE ANCIENT CITY

Although rich in legend and history, Corfu is relatively poor in archaeological remains. Palaeopolis, or ancient Corcyra, faced the mainland of Epirus and controlled the narrow coastal straits from the military port at Anemomilos (Fig 7). Corcyra's acropolis stood near the modern village of Analipsis and the aristocratic part of the town lay on the slope now largely occupied by the park of Mon Repos. The town square or agora is believed to have been situated at the foot of the slope near the

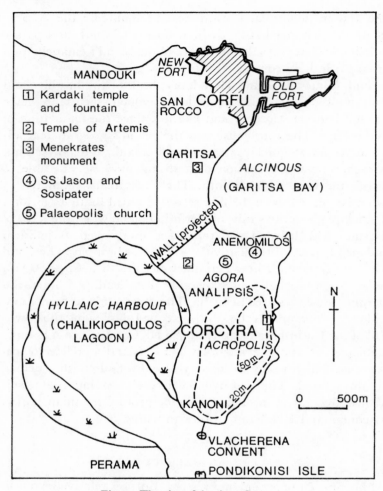

Fig 7   The site of Ancient Corcyra

eastward-facing of the two harbours. Excavations in 1965 revealed part of the ancient seawall. In the fifth century BC a defensive wall ran across the northern neck of the peninsula from Chalikiopoulos (the Hyllaic harbour) to Garitsa Bay (Alcinous), although its precise alignment has not been determined except for a small section in the south-west which was revealed in 1812.

Certain archaeological discoveries enable the fortunes of Corcyra to be traced, but it is interesting that there is no evidence of occupation of this site prior to 734 BC. Therefore the Palaeopolis peninsula is not a valid contestant for the site of the Phaecaean capital. Some Corinthian pottery from the city's earliest years has been unearthed and also from later in the seventh century, but the most important discoveries are structural ruins dating from the sixth century. Sir George Wheeler's account of ancient Corcyra in 1675 stresses the 'abundance of ruins and foundations'. But from the Middle Ages until the beginning of the eighteenth century Corcyra was used as a building quarry for the medieval town which was developed to the north. An estimated 20,000 stones were used chiefly in the construction of the Venetian fortifications. The site also lost many of its artistic relics to private collections and museums in Europe, including the British Museum where the precedent set by Lord Elgin was repeated. What little remains on the island is now housed in Corfu's archaeological museum and the prize exhibit is the partly restored west pediment of the Temple of Artemis. This was discovered in 1911 during an excavation supervised by Dorpfeld and financed by Kaiser Wilhelm II.

The pediment is dominated by a central figure of a colossal gorgon, 9ft high, whose face is portrayed with a frightful grin, bared teeth, protruding tongue and snakes for hair and belt. Her knees are bent in profile, the archaic convention for rapid running. She is flanked by her sons – offsprings who came to life from her dying blood. On the left was a rampant Pegasus, but all that remains are his forefoot resting on her arm, his hindquarters and part of his wings. On her left is Chrysaor of the golden sword with a bestial grin, obviously inherited! The group is flanked by heraldic beasts, part lion, part panther. These are orientalising in style with the left one fierce and the right one placid. The pediment angles depict Zeus striking down a Titan with a thunderbolt, and an outstretched dead Titan.

The full significance of the pediment sculptures are lost in pagan mythology but in all probability they are apotropaic, that is they were carved to ward off evil powers from the temple and its contents and have nothing to do with the myths and worship of Artemis. The pediment's interest rests not so much in its meaning as in the fact that it represents an example of early Corinthian art dating back to the beginning of the sixth century BC. It is probably the oldest peripetal temple of stone in the Doric mainland style for few other specimens were saved after the Roman destruction of Corinth in 146 BC.

The Temple of Artemis was discovered during the French occupation of Corfu when General Donzelot excavated the ancient city moat to add to the town's southern defences. Under the patronage of Kaiser Wilhelm II more systematic studies were carried out by Dorpfeld between 1911 and 1914. The building, measuring 42·14m by 22·56m, was externally constructed of limestone and followed the Doric order. In 520 BC its terracotta tiles, cima and antefixes were replaced by fittings in Parian marble. Further work since World War II revealed that the temple was the focal point in a complex of public buildings. There is also evidence of another temple of Artemis at the southern tip of the peninsula and in 1889 Karapanos uncovered clay votives of the seventh century depicting the goddess and her lions. Further fragments of this temple were discovered by Dorpfeld in 1912. Other Doric remains include the temple and fountain of Kardaki. Here water was once channelled through the precincts of the sanctuary whose ruins lie in Mon Repos park. The park also contains the remains of the Heraion, a temple mentioned by Thucydides.

The cemetery of ancient Corcyra lay outside the town in the area now occupied by the modern suburb of Garitsa. The Tomb of Menekrates, discovered in 1846, commemorates the Consul of Oeanthe in Locris who was drowned at sea. It is a tumulus measuring a little over 5yd across by nearly 2yd high and is surrounded by a circular base of carved stones. Near the tomb the so-called Lion of Menekrates was discovered, reputed to be one of the most beautiful animal sculptures in early Greece. Experts differ on its date but place it between 620 and 550 BC. There is also some controversy as to whether or not it was associated with the tomb.

THE PELOPONNESIAN WAR

It would be misleading to suggest that Corcyra was in any way the real cause of the Peloponnesian War, yet the island was 'the apple of discord' that ultimately led to the great conflict between Athens and Sparta. Its origins developed from a dispute between Corinth and Corcyra over the small city state of Epidamnus which in 435 BC was involved in civil war. The controlling democrats of the city were hard-pressed by the oligarchs and it appears that Corcyraean sympathies were with the latter. Corinth, in support of the democrats, sent settlers overland and troops from Corinth, Lefkas and Ambracia. Thucydides records in detail the Corinthian motives which revealed a typically Greek blending of sentiment and material interest.

> Believing the colony to belong as much to themselves as to the Corcyraeans, they [the Corinthians] felt it to be a kind of duty to undertake its protection. Besides they hated the Corcyraeans for their neglect of the mother-city. Instead of meeting with the usual honours accorded to the parent-city by every colony at public assemblies, such as precedence at sacrifices, Corinth found herself treated with contempt by a power which in point of wealth could stand comparison with the richest Greek states of the day

and 'which possessed a great military strength . . . whose nautical renown dated from the days of Homer's Phaecaeans'.

Corinth enlarged the area of conflict by offering a place in Epidamnus to any volunteers and by asking other states to assist in the democratic cause. Promises of vessels, troops and money were received from Megara, Thebes, Epidaurus, Ermione, Troezen, Elis and Pale in Cefalonia – states which were eager to re-establish naval control in the Ionian Sea. Corcyra reacted violently to Corinthian intervention and the reinforcements for Epidamnus, conveyed in a fleet of seventy-five Corinthian and allied ships, were defeated by eighty Corcyraean ships off the Ambracian Gulf. Epidamnus surrendered, the cities which supported Corinth were plundered by the Corcyraeans, and many prisoners were executed or sold as slaves. Corcyra now acquired temporary control of the Ionian Sea, but the city was committed to war with a number of Peloponnesian states.

For two years Corinth increased the size and efficiency of its navy, and Corcyra, lacking in Greek allies, sent envoys to Athens to negotiate a treaty. Corinth counteracted with its own representatives to dissuade Athens from granting an alliance. Thucydides describes the cases stated by both parties and two days of debate passed before Athens reached a decision.

> The general belief was that, whatever happened, war with the Peloponnesus was bound to come. Athens had no wish to see the strong navy of Corcyra pass into Corinthian hands. At the same time Athens was not averse to letting the two powers weaken each other in warfare since in this way, if war did come, Athens would be stronger in relation to Corinth and to other naval powers. Then, too, it was a fact that Corcyra lay conveniently on the coastal route to Italy and Sicily.

Swayed by the advice of Pericles, a defensive rather than offensive alliance was made with Corcyra. Corcyra was not an ally of Sparta and a defensive alliance in no way broke the non-aggression pact between Athens and Corinth, the latter a member of the Spartan Alliance.

In 433 BC a second battle was fought between Corcyra and Corinth off the Sybota Isles. Corinth sailed with a fleet of 150 ships under the leadership of Admiral Xenoclides. The Corcyraeans manned 110 ships of which 10 were a token-force from Athens. 'The fighting', states Thucydides, 'was of a somewhat old-fashioned kind . . . both sides having a number of hoplites aboard their ships, together with archers and javelin throwers. But the fighting was hard enough, in spite of the lack of skill shown: indeed, it was more like a battle on land than a naval engagement.' Corcyra lost 70 ships and Corinth and her allies would have been victorious had not a further 20 ships arrived from Athens to reinforce the original 10. This succeeded in routing the Corinthians and the battle was regarded as the greatest fought at sea between Greek and Greek. The seas were strewn with the wreckage of 100 triremes and the bodies of several thousand seamen.

The immediate results were inconclusive, but both Corinth and her ally Megara were members of the Spartan Confederacy and the engagement between Athens and the cities under Spartan protection inevitably brought the two great powers face to face. The Athenian navy was largely intact and in Corcyra Athens had a strong base for operations against the Peloponnesus and a staging-point on the passage to Sicily and Italy. In the months that followed the battle of Sybota, Athens aggravated the situation by issuing economic sanctions against Megara and by presenting an ultimatum to Potidaea, a colony of Corinth, to break its ties with the mother-city. The negotiations which led to war are of extreme complexity but by 431 BC most of the city states were engaged in a conflict which lasted twenty-seven years, broken only by a few brief intervals of truce. The Peloponnesian War marked the turning-point in the history of the Greek city state and its effects of Corcyra, the unsuspecting 'instigator' of the conflict, were tragic.

CIVIL WAR AND TYRANTS

Corcyra's decline in political power and prestige is perhaps best illustrated from Thucydides' *Peloponnesian Wars*. In the last five of the eight books that make up the history the Corcyraeans, who were given so much attention in the earlier sections, are hardly mentioned. In 427 BC Corcyra was split by civil strife into two factions, the democrats who favoured Athens and the oligarchs who supported the Spartan alliance. This situation was of major concern to Athens and Sparta for its outcome was capable of swinging the balance of power in the west. When bloody revolution broke out on the island both Athenian and Peloponnesian ships came to the aid of the opposing factions. The Peloponnesians ravaged the southern promontory of the island but the Athenian fleet lay in Corcyra harbour while the democrats proceeded to slaughter the oligarchs. The personal hatred is related by Thucydides who, although sympathetic to the democratic and Athenian cause, did not condone the acts of savagery. 'There were fathers who killed sons; men were dragged from the temples and butchered on the very altars; some were actually walled up in the temple and died there.' Many oligarchs escaped to the mainland and occupied strategic positions across the channel where they waged a guerrilla war for two years until the Athenians intervened. The horrors of Corcyra spread to almost all the Greek world and the wheel of revolution was kept spinning in the fourth century by the rise and fall of imperialistic powers. Throughout the Peloponnesian War the Corcyraeans were active at sea and together with fleets from Cefalonia, Zakinthos and Cythera, they joined the Athenian expedition to Syracuse, a major source of Corinthian revenue.

Thucydides makes no further mention of Corcyra after the fall of Syracuse, but the story is taken up by Xenophon. At the beginning of the fourth century it appears that an aristocratic party with a strict policy of neutrality emerged in Corcyra but quickly fell under Spartan domination. In 377 BC, however, the island joined the second Athenian confederacy and was besieged by a powerful Spartan fleet under the leadership of Mnasippos. Aided by a revolt among the Spartan mercenaries, the Corcyraeans made a successful stand, Mnasippos was killed and the siege lifted. Xenophon then records the island as a 'paradise of fertility and cultivation' where the invaders 'glutted their bodies with grain, fruit, oxen and women'!

The protracted period of political unrest and bloodshed considerably weakened the strength of Corcyra and during the fourth century BC it was involved in the turbulent conditions which saw the rise of Macedon and the political decline of Athens. For most of the third century the island bereft of powerful allies, was ruled by a series of tyrants and subjected to invasions from Sicily, Illyria and Epirus.

ROMAN INTERVENTION

It is a generally accepted view of historians that Rome had no positive eastern policy for the Mediterranean until after 200 BC. The empire's gradual involvement in Greek affairs was largely fortuitous and unpremeditated, and was not the outcome of a conscious design to expand its boundaries politically. Although there was no large-scale military entanglement prior to 214 BC, contact between Rome and the eastern Mediterranean developed in the form of a subtle political liaison similar to the principles of an *entente cordiale*. Informal and friendly connections with free states, especially those strategically situated, formed the basis of Roman involvement which rested on the recognition of the independence of weaker states. Intervention into their affairs came only when the future of such states became a political threat to Rome's economic integrity.

It was the Illyrians, under the leadership of Queen Teuta, who brought the Romans to Corcyra, which was the first of the Greek cities to submit to the western power. Illyrian pirates were well on the way to acquiring control of the Adriatic coasts and islands and thus the approaches to Sicily and Italy from the Ionian Islands. Initially the Corcyraeans and the inhabitants of Epidamnus and Apollonia appealed to the Greek states for assistance, but the Aetolian and Achaean Leagues which reached Paxos were defeated by the Illyrians. Rome intervened by sending a fleet of 200 ships to Corcyra and Demetrius, who had been left in charge of the island with an Illyrian garrison, surrendered to Rome in 229 BC. Rome then proceeded to Apollonia where an army of 20,000 infantry and 2,000 cavalry arrived from Brindisi. Corcyra, recognising the importance of a powerful defender with forces larger than anything the Greek leagues could provide, placed itself under Roman protection.

Rome treated the Greeks with moderation and to a certain degree Corcyra remained a free state governed by its own laws and electing its own magistrates. As a Roman protectorate the island commercially thrived, both as a result of its fertility and of its position as a strategic port of call between the Roman and Greek worlds. It also became a principal naval base for Roman expansion into Macedonia and Greece and during the latter decades of the Republic it was inevitably embroiled in the various power-struggles between provinces and political parties.

Roman remains are even fewer than those for the pre-Roman era. There are some foundations of baths and mosaic pavements at Palaeopolis and Benitses but Roman names connected with the island are numerous, for Greek civilisation and its artistic achievements appealed strongly to the Roman upper classes. The island's natural beauty attracted a number of Roman emperors. Tiberius is said to have had a summer residence at Kassiopi and Corfu provided the winter quarters for the consuls during the Macedonian wars. Cato, Cicero, Antony, Octavia and Agrippina are other names associated with the island and Nero was as attracted by the arts and scenery of Corcyra as he was to other parts of Greece. Nero, not content with sculpture, yearned to display his 'manifold talents' before a Greek audience, 'the only one', he said, 'worthy of himself and his accomplishments'. In AD 66 he crossed over to Kassiopi and, according to Suetonius, began his theatrical tour by playing and singing before the altar of Jupiter Cassius. There are a number of references that Kassiopi in the north-east of the island was a centre of considerable importance during Roman times. No traces of the temple remain but its name lives on in that of the modern village.

4

THE PAWN IN A
MEDIEVAL GAME

THE Roman occupation of Corfu virtually put an end to
the island's independence and throughout the medieval
period geographical position was again to rule its destiny.
The island was the natural stepping-stone on the route from
southern Italy to mainland Greece, the guardian of the entrance to the Strait of Otranto and the key to the Adriatic sea
route. Strategic significance made it a prize for which the
dominant powers of the eastern Mediterranean and the Italian
peninsula competed from the eleventh century onwards –
Byzantium, the Despotate of Epirus and the Ottoman Turks on
the one hand, Venice, the Normans and the Angevins on the
other. Corfu was tossed like a ball between empires and principalities, becoming a pawn in the power-politics of the period
and in the struggle for supremacy between the eastern and
western Mediterranean. The variety of detail in the island's
medieval history, yet the stubborn sameness of its general
pattern, emphasises its traditional function both as a boundary
stone and intermediary between West and East. The centuries
of coexistence between Latin and Hellenic values, between
Catholicism and Orthodoxy, have left a permanent mark on
the island's contemporary character.

ROME, EAST AND WEST

The beginning of the medieval period is traditionally accepted
as coinciding with the fall of the Roman empire in the West.
In AD 285, Diocletian, for military and administrative con-

venience, divided the empire into eastern and western halves in line with the division between Greek and Latin populations. His residence became Nicomedia, near the Sea of Marmora. Early in the next century the empire was reunited under Constantine, but the capital Constantinople was fixed in the east on the site of the ancient Greek colony of Byzantium. The strategic position of Constantinople at the southern extremity of the Bosphorus marked a new era in the history of the Mediterranean, for it ultimately led to a fundamental separation of the empire's eastern and western provinces. Where one emperor had formerly ruled from Rome, now two imperial colleagues, ruling jointly, shared the growing burdens of government: in the west one resided at Rome, Milan, Ravenna or Trèves, whilst in the east Constantinople (but sometimes Antioch) became the capital of the other.

The fates of the two empires were very different. Under the assaults of successive barbarian invasions the highly organised western frontier collapsed, but the eastern empire, the territories of which took the name Byzantine, survived into the thirteenth century and in part until 1453. From the fall of Rome (AD 476) to that of Constantinople (1453) the Byzantine empire was a constantly changing political expression, but its main function was that of a bulwark for Europe against Asiatic aggression. The highly civilised state was the repository and inheritor of the Graeco–Roman culture that had dominated the Mediterranean.

Constantinople was quick to reap the benefits of its incomparable site. Standing at the intersection of arterial routes, by land from Thrace and Asia Minor and by water from the Aegean and Black Seas, the city drew to itself the economic and intellectual activities of the eastern Mediterranean. Controlled commerce, however, and a centrally directed administration meant that the imperial city grew at the expense of many parts of its empire, and Greece in particular failed to recover the prosperity and importance it had enjoyed in the Mediterranean prior to the rise of Rome. Within the empire it occupied a

Venetian memorials:
Plate 9 (right) The elegantly decorated well of Kremasti, built in 1699
Plate 10 (below) The Lion of St Mark on a western rampart of the New Fort

Plate 11 Nineteenth-century Corfu: The Old Fort and the town viewed from the bay. (*Nineteenth Century Prints*)

Plate 12 The Royal Road in 1840 illustrating a mixture of traditional European costumes. (*Nineteenth Century Prints*)

provincial status – often a cultural and economic backwater – and its coasts and islands became the goals for piecemeal conquests by expansionist states to the north and west. Ultimately Byzantium's energies were spent in the battle for survival against both European and Asiatic forces. Primarily it was a sea-state in the sense that the unity of its possessions were preserved by a navy that played a salient role in the medieval history of the Mediterranean.

Corfu was one of Byzantium's most westerly possessions and became the foremost stronghold against both barbarians and Franks. The island was vital in maintaining contact with Byzantine possessions in Apulia and Sicily, but its exposed position inevitably involved it in a series of barbarian attacks. The earliest recorded raids are those by Genseric, an ally of Attila the Hun. These occurred in AD 441 and were followed in AD 445 by the Vandals. After devastating Rome the Ostrogoths under Totila ravaged the island in AD 562 with a fleet of 300 galleys. Vigorous and successful attempts were made by the Emperor Justinian to regain some of the western lands but between AD 587 and AD 805 the Slavs and Bulgars both raided and settled on Corfu. Tradition records Arsenios, Metropolitan of Corfu, as being rescued from Bulgar hands by the valour of the islanders. In consequence of the repeated barbarian attacks the Byzantine settlement was moved from the site of ancient Corcyra to the double-pronged rock to the north. This defensive position became a fortified *castro*, the nucleus of the later medieval town.

With the exception of its invaders, few other details are known about the development of Corfu in the early centuries AD, although there are scant references to the victory of Christianity which was to transform the character of the Roman empire. The fourth century saw the gradual establishment of the new religion and the privileged position of the Church, which a generation earlier had suffered its fiercest persecution. Corfu had its own early Christian martyrs in Jason and Sosipatros, Bishops of Tarsus and Iconium, whose

D

deaths by burning around AD 200 are commemorated in the twelfth-century church at Anemomilos. The harmony between Christian teaching and pagan cults was temporarily disrupted under the rule of Julian who fostered the ancient religion with its caesar-worship. The triumph of paganism ended with the successions of Jovian and Valens and on Corfu the former ordered the erection of the Church of the Virgin on the site of a heathen temple. Its ruins, consisting of a belfry and four standing walls, lie to the north-east of the entrance to Mon Repos. Known as Palaeopolis church it is the oldest Christian edifice on the island and dates *c* AD 555.

VENETIANS AND NORMANS

The efforts by Byzantium to retain control of Corfu were largely successful until the late eleventh century. The western approaches to Greece, however, were coveted by the expansionist states and kingdoms of Europe, and although the imperial capital maintained *de jure* sovereignty over its Adriatic and Ionian possessions, it was geographically inevitable that *de facto* control passed to other powers.

The location of Venice at the head of the Adriatic and between the eastern and western halves of the Mediterranean permitted it to function at an early date as an intermediary between the Greek East and the Latin West. From the late seventh century its merchants were attracted by the splendours of Constantinople and the opportunities it offered for trade and commerce. The Venetian rise to power was the product of political independence – the gift of its island sites – but the city also shrewdly accepted a formal Byzantine suzerainty under cover of which it was able to monopolise East–West trade. By the eleventh century the Byzantine emperors had come to regard Venice as an independent ally, according lofty titles to the Doges and a place in the hierarchy of the Greek imperial court. Venice in return rendered valuable military service to Byzantium and was granted trading rights within the empire and a virtually independent Venetian colony in Constantinople. Extensive as these commercial privileges were Venice soon sought control of the entire lucrative trade of Byzantium. A series of events in the eleventh century formed major steps to Venice's long-term objectives.

In 1071 Normans, seeking to match the exploits of William the Conqueror in England, began the piecemeal conquest of Byzantine southern Italy and Sicily. This was to take all of twenty years and their ultimate ambition was to seize Constantinople. Among the Norman adventurers, whose careers developed from mercenary soldiers to independent chiefs, were ten brothers, four of which were successively elected Counts of Apulia: William the Iron Arm, Drogo, Humphrey and Robert. The last, surnamed Guiscard (the Wizard), was a powerful soldier-statesman and Byzantium's most dangerous enemy. His realm in southern Italy appears small on historical maps but this belies its importance, for outside of Islam and Byzantium it was the first state in southern Europe to be effectively organised since the fall of Rome.

Dissatisfied with his Italian conquests Guiscard attempted to gain a foothold on Greek soil by offering the hand of his daughter Helena to the son of the deposed emperor Michael VII Ducas (1071–8). The matrimonial plans failed and after extensive preparations Guiscard sailed from Brindisi in June 1081 with an army of 30,000 men and 150 ships. Corfu, which then yielded an annual revenue of 1,500lb of gold to the Byzantine treasury, surrendered to Guiscard and he landed in Epirus unopposed. His victories were checked by troubles in Italy and in 1082 he returned leaving his son Bohemund in command of his armies. In the following year the emperor Alexius I Comnenus (1081–1118), taking full advantage of Norman discontent, counter-attacked and successfully freed a number of Greek territories. Guiscard prepared for another expedition in 1084, but with the aid of Venice the Byzantine fleet defeated him off Corfu – although not without the loss of 13,000 men. Guiscard's unexpected death in 1085 led to the

Norman evacuation of all Greek territories and this provided the opportunity Venice had long awaited. The Venetian price for maritime assistance in Byzantium's battles unrestricted free trade throughout the empire, with special commercial privileges in Athens, Thebes, Corinth, Nauplia, Methone and above all in Corfu.

The Norman conquests in southern Italy were consolidated by Guiscard's nephew, Roger II of Sicily, who brought the Kingdom of Sicily to the zenith of its power by the annexation of Naples (1150) and the Zirid emirates of Tunisia (1134–53). The Normans returned to Corfu in 1147 and the rapid control of the island by the Sicilian Admiral, George of Antioch, was aided by the islanders insurrection against heavy Byzantine taxes. Venice again came to Byzantium's rescue and after a long siege in 1149 which won the admiration of the Norman commander the island was returned to the Emperor Manuel I Comnenus (1143–80). Venetian trading privileges were further extended to Rhodes and Cyprus, but thereafter relations between Venice and Constantinople deteriorated. The Venetians were opposed to Manuel acquiring territory in southern Italy and joined forces with William I against the Byzantine expedition to Apulia. Byzantium turned for assistance to Pisa and Genoa, Venice's commercial rivals: thus trading concessions, including quarters in Constantinople, were granted to these cities.

The third Norman attack on Corfu was launched in 1182 when the island was taken by Margaritone, the piratical admiral of William II. Corfu was returned to Byzantium in a peace treaty of 1187, but Venetian antagonism continued, ultimately leading to the fall of Constantinople to the Franks in 1204. Prior to this Corfu was seized by Leone Vetrano, a Genoese pirate – 'the terror of the Greek seas'. His exploits were supported by Genoa in the hope of disrupting Venetian commerce. Genoa was Venice's only major rival and although diplomatic and trading relations existed between them, at heart they were mortal enemies.

THE FOURTH CRUSADE

The ambition of displacing all western merchants from a share in the rich Greek markets motivated Venetian participation in the Fourth Crusade. It had been preached in Western Europe from the end of 1199 and became the crowning glory of the pontificate of Innocent II. As the principal maritime power, the leaders applied to Venice to furnish their armies which were to number 9,000 knights, 20,000 foot soldiers and 4,500 horses. The Doge, Dandolo, agreed to provide warships and merchantmen for a sum of 34,000 silver marks and for half of all the conquered territories. Venice also agreed to supply and victual the army for a period of one year. The crusaders' inability to pay the agreed sum of money on time drastically changed the original plans which were directed against the Moslems. Dandolo proposed the deferment of the payment on condition that the armies should first reduce the Adriatic city of Zara which had rebelled against Venice and admitted a Hungarian garrison. Zara was taken in 1202 and the pope excommunicated both the crusaders and the Republic of Venice for 'turning the swords they had consecrated to the service of Christianity against Christians'.

The Zara campaign was a preliminary to a much greater diversion in which Venetian manipulation led to the final perversion of the whole enterprise. This was to lead to a move against Constantinople, rather than against the Moslem 'infidel'. In a treaty the crusaders agreed to place the deposed Issac II and his son Alexius on the Byzantine throne and it was further agreed to place the Eastern Church under papal authority. Venice had everything to gain from an attack on its great commercial rival and in 1203 the crusading armada lay off Corfu while the plans for Constantinople were finalised.

Corfu was an important refurbishing point on the crusaders' route to and from the East. Richard, Coeur de Lion, had landed in 1192 on his return from the Third Crusade, but often the island suffered under the hands of the Christians as in 1112, when it was raided by Pisans *en route* to reinforce the Latin Kingdom of Jerusalem. Geoffrey de Villehardoun, the historian of the Fourth Crusade, regarded the sight of the fleet as it left Corfu as the greatest experience of his youth. 'It was a more wonderful sight than has ever been seen before. As far as the eye could reach, the sea was covered with sails of ships and galleys. Our hearts were filled with joy and we felt that our armament could undertake the conquest of the world.'

The successful attack on the eastern bastion of Christianity by knights, supposedly on their way to protect the Church and harass the Moslems, was an act that made the Fourth Crusade infamous and one which earned for it the title of the 'greatest commercial *coup*' of all times. It also effected greater changes in Greece than any event since the Roman conquest. Once in possession of Constantinople the crusaders were involved in disputes over the imperial throne which were partially resolved by the division of the empire and its spoils amongst themselves. The first Latin Emperor of Constantinople was Count Baldwin of Flanders who ruled over a restricted territory known as Romania, lying athwart the Sea of Marmora. The remainder of the empire was divided half to the crusaders and half to Venice. Boniface de Montferrat, Commander-in-Chief of the crusaders, became 'King of Salonica' through a grant of land which included Macedonia, Thessaly and much of central Greece. To the south the Lordship of Athens passed to Othon de la Roche, a Burgundian noble and an associate of Boniface.

From the commercial point of view Venice secured the choicest of the Greek areas. It acquired three-quarters of Constantinople, most of the Aegean and Ionian islands, Crete, Euboea and several important points in the Peloponnesus, including the strategic fortresses of Modon and Cronon. These possessions were the stepping-stones of the Venetian sea-state – a series of defensive sites, calling-stations and merchant quarters in cities strung along the major medieval trade routes. Realising the difficulties of directly administrating these territories, grants of land and dependencies were awarded to Venetian nobles in return for trade privileges within them. Zante, Cefalonia and Ithaca were governed by Matthew Orosini as the County Palatine of Cefalonia, but Corfu and Paxos were still controlled by Leone Vetrano. The Venetians had no intention of leaving these islands in the hands of a Genoese pirate and in 1205 the fleet which bore Thomas Morosini, the first Latin Patriarch of Constantinople, formally took possession of Corfu. It was placed under the direct authority of the Commune of Venice. The islanders had strongly supported the independent spirit of Vetrano and his reappearance was welcomed with enthusiasm. In 1206 a large Venetian fleet commanded by Dandolo's son again took Corfu and Vetrano and his partisans were executed.

In 1207 the island and its dependencies were transferred to the care of ten Venetian nobles on conditions that they maintained the garrisons and paid the Republic an annuity of 500 gold pieces. Special concessions were awarded to Venetian merchants and the rights of the Greeks were protected as long as they remained loyal to Venice. The Orthodox Church was respected and taxes were not raised beyond the dues the Corfiotes were accustomed to pay under Byzantium. Venice hoped that these measures would gain the loyalty of the islanders and firmly secure the possession of Corfu.

THE DESPOTATE OF EPIRUS

The initial Venetian occupation of Corfu was of short duration. The dismemberment of the Byzantine empire produced a succession of states in the provinces whose rulers vied with each other in their campaigns against the common Frankish enemy. In Asia Minor, Theodore Lascaris, a relative of the last reigning dynasty in Constantinople, established a court at Nicaea and ruled as 'emperor in exile'. He claimed to be the lawful heir to the throne and Nicaea became the centre of a revived Greek empire. In western Greece a serious rival to Nicaea was

Michael Angelos Comnenus, another representative of the imperial family and first cousin of Issac I. Michael's Despotate of Epirus (Arta or Hellas as it was variously called) developed from a mere resistance movement into a powerful kingdom extending from Durazzo in the north to Naupaktos on the Gulf of Patras in the south (Fig 8). It became the centre of Greek patriotism amidst the Latin states and the court at Arta was a refuge for Greeks throughout the Balkan peninsula and the

Fig 8 . Central Greece in the thirteenth century

islands. Epirus was saved from Latin feudal domination and its civil government was a continuation of Byzantine forms.

The existence of a neighbouring Greek state proved a great attraction for the Corfiotes and when in 1214 Michael seized the island from the Venetian nobles, the Corfiotes willingly threw off the Latin yoke and became his loyal subjects. The island prospered under the Despotate and the wealth of its merchants, traders and landowners enabled Michael to maintain a respectable army of mercenaries. Great care was taken to foster the support of the Corfiotes for monetary burdens were reduced for the laity and the privileges of the Church were ratified and extended. Orthodoxy became the strongest ally of the Despotate and from the scant sources available for the period the Corfiote Church reached its zenith in prestige. Basil Pediates, the Metropolitan of Corfu (1204–9), claimed direct connection with the Patriarchate of Constantinople and attempted to free orthodoxy from the influences of catholicism. He waged a verbal war against the pope and questioned the Roman Church's 'foolish ideas over the sacraments and the procession of the Holy Spirit'. His successor, George Bardanes, continued the battle and was nominated Metropolitan of Corfu at the Arta synod in 1219.

Michael I distinguished himself as a soldier and a negotiator. He extended his authority to all Epirus, Acarnania, Aetolia and parts of Macedonia and Thrace. But his conquests and governmental career were abruptly terminated in 1215 by his assassination by one of his slaves. The Despotate was then ruled by his brothers Theodor (1215–30) and Manuel (1230–7), although the latter's rule in Epirus remains obscure. Michael's young son was sent into exile in the Peloponnesus, but fifteen years later he returned to claim his heritage. The special concessions granted to Corfu by his father were reinstigated and in 1256 Michael II exempted both the townspeople and the peasants from taxation. Like his father he attached the greatest importance to fostering the loyalty of the Corfiotes and two further chrysobulls were introduced. The first confirmed and extended the privileges of the thirty-two town priests who, under the name of the 'Sacred Bond' formed a religious college or corporation, and the second granted the rural clergy with similar privileges to form a closed corporation known as 'Freemen'. These concessions upheld the position of orthodoxy and secured Corfu as a loyal mandate of Epirus. The old civil administration of ten demarchies, instituted by the Venetians, was also modified.

MANFRED OF SICILY

The success of the Despotate alarmed the Franks and offended the rival Greek empire of Nicaea. In his struggle for Greek leadership Michael II unsuccessfully tried to gain the friendship and support of the German Emperor Frederick II. On Frederick's death in 1250 his bastard son Manfred was granted the Principality of Taranto and was recognised as the baillie of the Kingdom of Sicily by Conrad, Frederick's legitimate successor. Manfred refused to accept the autocracy of the pope and inherited many of the ambitions of his Norman predecessors. During Michael II's campaign against Nicaea, a Sicilian fleet seized a large part of the Albanian and north Epirot coast, including the towns of Avlona and Durazzo. Philip Chinardo, a Cypriot Frank attached to Manfred's cause, extended the conquests southwards and in June 1258 Corfu, the Sybota Isles, Butrinto and Chimara were taken.

The losses of Durazzo and Corfu were bitter blows to Michael, but he wisely considered it more politic to come to terms with Manfred rather than weaken his own resources by disputing Manfred's claims to the Epirot conquests. An alliance was proposed, the bribe being the hand of Michael's eldest daughter, Helena. Her dowry, which included Corfu, was already in Manfred's possession. The arrangement was convenient to both parties: for Manfred it saved him from maintaining an active foothold in Greece and for Michael it meant that undivided attention could be directed against

Nicaea. Manfred proved a useful but unfortunately short-lived ally to Michael's campaigns in Greece. The move against Naples and Sicily by Charles of Anjou forced Manfred to return. In 1266 Charles, supported by the pope, was victorious in the Battle of Benevento, where Manfred was killed.

Manfred's Corfu and mainland possessions were entrusted to Chinardo who by virtue of being ruler bestowed Corfiote fiefs on his lieutenants. Helena was imprisoned by Charles and the Corfu dowry was given to Maria, Michael's sister-in-law. She in turn was offered to Chinardo, a benevolent but crafty move on Michael's part which culminated in Chinardo's assassination by a party of Corfiotes who supported the Despotate. Corfu and the Epirot coast were returned to Michael II for a brief period, but Garnier Aleman (the inheritor of the Barony of Patras from the Frankish conquest of the Peloponnesus) had strong motives for curbing further Greek expansion. For assistance he turned to his fellow countryman, Charles of Anjou, who already regarded himself as the rightful successor to Manfred's Greek dominions. The Treaty of Viterbo (1267) formally recognised Charles's rights to Corfu, and Aleman, in recognition of his services, was appointed governor of the island. On the death of Michael II the Despotate was divided between his sons: John Doucas established himself at Neopatras, and Nikephoros at Arta. Under the Palaeologus family the Empire of Nicaea gained the Byzantine prize with the recapture of Constantinople in 1261. The court of Arta, however, continued to preserve its patriotic identity and clung to the illusion that its rulers held an equal claim to the Byzantine throne.

THE ANGEVINS

Charles of Anjou's grand ambition was to retake Constantinople for the Latin Emperor Baldwin II. His plans, conceived at Viterbo and foreshadowing those of Napoleon Bonaparte five centuries later, considered Corfu to be the first step in the conquest of the East. In 1272 Giordano di San Felice replaced

Aleman and controlled the island from its three main fortresses – Castel Vecchio and Castel Nuovo (the two fortified summits of the Old Fort) and Saint Angelo. The latter was built by Michael I at Palaeokastritsa to guard against Genoese pirates. The fortresses of Sybota and Butrinto were also under Felice's command.

The Angevin plans for Constantinople were short-lived for in 1282 the Sicilian Vespers drove the House of Anjou from Sicily and the kingdom was handed to the rival house of Aragon. The fortunes of Corfu were indirectly affected for the island was now exposed to attacks from the Aragonese fleet. There are recorded raids by Roger de Lluria, Berenguer d'Entenca and Berenguer Villaraut and *en route* to Constantinople Corfu was plundered by the Catalan Grand Company.

The prestige and position of Charles of Anjou rested on papal support and he repaid this obligation by propagating catholicism among his orthodox subjects. The Metropolitan of Corfu was deposed and his title was replaced by the less-dignified term *protopappas* or chief priest. Monastic lands were seized and the orthodox cathedral and churches were controlled by the catholic clergy. The Angevins, however, were more tolerant to the Jews and a Corfiote ghetto and synagogue are first mentioned in 1365. Successive Angevin rulers offered protection and inducement to the settlement of Levantine and Italian Jews.

Corfiote local government was radically altered. A viceroy was appointed, directly responsible to the king, and the island was divided into four bailiwicks each with its own court. A treasurer and inquisitor completed the governmental officials and a high court of justice operated with Latin as the official language. Corfiote life was forced to follow the feudal tenor of the age and land was divided between the ruler's domain, church estates, feudal fiefs and barons. Economically and strategically the island was valuable to the Angevins. It possessed salt pans, produced an abundance of wine, and its olive trees provided a rich source of income. It appears that Corfu was also well-suited for horse-rearing and towards the end of the fourteenth century a special fief was granted to encourage the settlement of gypsies on account of their equestrian skills.

Not a lot is known of the fortunes of Corfu between 1294 and 1373, except for the names of its sovereigns – Charles II, Philip I, Robert, Philip II of Taranto, Catharine of Valois and Marie of Bourbon. The island then experienced a period of disputed rights involving Jacques de Baux, the nephew of Philip II, and Queen Joanna I of Naples. Joanna held possession of the island for seven years, but in 1380 it was attacked by mercenaries in the pay of de Baux. Joanna lost both crown and life when Charles of Durazzo attacked Naples and thereby acquired Corfu. His death in 1386, together with the decline of the Angevin dynasty, left the island easy prey to the expanding Serbian principalities to the north. As the only alternative the Corfiotes turned to Venice for protection.

In May 1386 an elected Corfiote envoy composed of Greeks, Italians and Jews presented a petition to the Venetian Republic. The island was offered to Venice provided that the Republic agreed to certain conditions. Chief of these were the confirmation of the privileges granted by earlier rulers, a declaration that Venice would not relinquish the island to any other power, and a promise that the system of fiefs would be maintained. The Corfiote deputation was warmly received for Venice had long been scheming to recover the island. On 8 January 1387 the terms of the contract were finalised but Venice, anxious to legalise its position, paid the sum of 30,000 gold ducats to Ladislaus, the *de facto* heir to Angevin Naples. This transaction ended Neapolitan claims to Corfu and with it their last connection with Greece. Neapolitan domination had strengthened the aristocracy and feudal system, both of which were to characterise Corfu for much of the Venetian period.

5   THE LION OF SAINT MARK

VENICE held unbroken possession of Corfu for 410 years (1387–1797). Thus the island was saved from the fate of mainland Greece and the Aegean by remaining free from Ottoman rule. The waves of the invading Turks lapped around Corfu and on two occasions tried to engulf it, but the island resisted and formed a boundary stone in the history of the Moslem conquest. Fynes Morison, writing in 1596, regarded it as 'one of the Chief Keys of Christendom', occupying a similar role to Rhodes in the east which was held by the Knights of St John. When other Greek lands fell to the Turks, Corfu grew rich as a centre of East–West trade, protected by the banner of Saint Mark, militant symbol of the Christian West. Together with its Ionian neighbours the island guarded the vital trade routes to Crete and Cyprus and it further enabled the Venetians to control the entire Adriatic. A text to the Senate (17 March 1550) called Corfu 'the heart' of the Venetian State and large sums of money were invested in its defences, sparing no expense says a document of 1553, *'che chi potesse veder li conti si stupiria'*. With Corfu and other strategic possessions the Turks were watched, if not walled in, by Venice's formidable line of fortresses and strong navy. The whole Republic's Levantine possessions were controlled by a powerful overlord capable of directing swift military action when needed.

VENETIAN ADMINISTRATION

The Venetians found the feudal system already in existence when they took over Corfu and true to the terms of the contract the new masters confirmed the Angevin barons in their fiefs.

Few new fiefs were created and their numbers dwindled from the original 24 to 12 or 15 at the end of the Venetian period, yet feudalism continued to form the basis of Corfiote society and the bulwark of Venetian rule. The island's administration, however, was modelled on that of the Republic and gradually a colonial superstructure was added to the feudal formations. For the first twenty-four years the government was entrusted to a single Venetian official who held office for two years under the title of 'bailie and captain'. In 1410 two councillors were sent from Venice to assist the bailie in civil and criminal jurisdiction and each received a yearly salary of 300 gold ducats and a house in Corfu town. The initial power of the bailie was further limited by the institution of a third office, the *provveditore e capitano*, appointed by the Venetian senate to carry out the duties of civil and military governor. He was both commander of the garrison and adjudicator on the finer points of feudal law and his jurisdiction extended over the barony of Paxos which the Venetians treated as an integral part of Corfu.

By the sixteenth century the powers of all Corfu's officials were overshadowed by those of the *provveditore generale del Levante*, first appointed during the Turkish war of 1499–1503. As well as commander of the fleet he was also a sort of governor-general appointed usually for three years. His arrival in Corfu was regulated by an elaborate code of pomp and etiquette. According to W. W. Miller, 'the Jews had to provide the carpets for the streets along which the great man would pass; the heads of both the Latin and Greek Churches greeted him with all the splendid rites of their respective establishments; a noble Corfiote pronounced a panegyric upon him in the Church of St Spiridon, before whose remains his excellency would kneel in prayer ere returning to his palace where obsequious Hebrews, laden with flowers, bent low as he crossed the threshold'. The *provveditore* and other officials were issued with strict orders to respect the rights of the islanders, and spies, known as 'inquisitors over the affairs of the Levant' were sent to Corfu from time to time to hear the grievances of the islanders. The Corfiotes often exercised the privilege of sending special missions to Venice to lay their complaints before the Doge.

The islanders, or rather those of noble birth, were granted a major share in the local administration. Society was divided into three classes – nobles, burghers and manual labourers, the latter including the peasantry. The first national council included many foreigners and local tradesmen but subsequent entrance was restricted and in 1440 the bailie was ordered by Venice to choose, on the advice of the local citizens, seventy prominent persons to form a communal or city council. This body was later increased to 150 – a total preserved until the last few years of Venetian rule when the council was reduced to sixty. The council of nobles was elected annually and formed a close oligarchy; it became the governing body of the island. It had the power of annually electing a number of *syndics* who were special representatives of the Corfiote community with the added role of price regulation in the markets. The council also appointed three judges and a number of purely honorary offices, the most prestigious of which was the *trierach*, or captain of the Corfiote war galleys. The town militia was controlled by the council of nobles and each rural community provided its own police force.

The *Libro d'Oro* was an imitation of a similar record at Venice and contained the names of the Corfiote nobles. New families from the burgher class were often added to this list, particularly after the Turkish siege of 1537 when the nobility was much reduced. Marmora (*Della Historia di Corfu*) writing in 1672 records the names of 112 noble families inscribed in the Golden Book. The document was burned as a symbol of class distinction when the French took Corfu in 1797.

Debarred from trade and compelled to reside in the town if they wished to play a part in the running of the island, the only employment open to the Corfiote aristocracy was either in the legal or administrative professions. These, however, afforded limited opportunities and 'very early in the Venetian period', stated Miller, 'we hear of the great number of Greek lawyers –

Plate 13 (right) Count von der Schulenburg, defender of the town against the Turkish siege of 1716

Plate 14 (below) Count John Capodistrias, Corfu's most famous son

Bell towers:
Plate 15 (left) St Spiridon's
square campanile is dated 1595
Plate 16 (below) An ornate
Greek-style belfry in the
Campiello quarter

then, as now, the plague of Greece'. The aristocracy's distaste for rural life resulted in agricultural neglect and on a number of occasions Corfu was threatened by famine. The peasants were practically serfs and had few political or legal rights. They were liable to forced labour on government works in the town and this led to major grievances, particularly when their labour was needed for farming duties such as sowing and harvesting. Many have argued that the condition of the peasantry was worse under the Venetian feudal system than many of their fellow Greeks on the mainland under Turkish rule. There are records of local peasant insurrections but it was not until the last century of Venetian rule that major troubles developed.

CATHOLIC AND ORTHODOX

Venice contented itself with the exercise of general control through its appointed agents, leaving the actual government of Corfu to the native aristocracy. Under this system Venetian rule was much less severe than that of the Angevins and its policies were particularly tolerant to the Greek Church and clergy. Whereas Venice gave precedence to the Catholic Church, it also realised that the interests of the Republic were of more importance than the papacy. Accordingly in Corfu, as in the Ionian Islands generally, they studiously prevented any encroachment on the part of either the Ecumenical patriarch or the pope. Venetian ecclesiastical policy is well expressed in an official document which stated 'that the Greeks should have liberty to preach and teach provided that they say nothing against the Republic and the Latin religion'.

The head of the Orthodox Church in Corfu was still titled the 'chief priest'. He was elected to his five-year appointment by a General Assembly but normally this election depended on his relationship and popularity with the noble families rather than on his personal merit. With a retinue of officials the chief priest enjoyed considerable honours and his decisions in ecclesiastical matters were rarely disputed. Communications with the

E

patriarch, however, were controlled and allowed only through the medium of the Venetian bailie at Constantinople.

The coveted title of archbishop was reserved for the head of the Catholic clergy, but there appears to have been little bitterness or rivalry between the two Churches. The Catholics took part in the religious festivals of the Orthodox, and the Greek clergy reciprocated by attending the special services and banquets of the Latin Churches. Interference with the religious rites of the Greeks was forbidden and with the introduction of the Gregorian calendar, Venice stipulated that Latins as well as Greeks should continue to use the old Julian reckoning on which the Orthodox year was based. Venice was aware, however, that politics and religion were inseparable to the Greeks and certain measures were taken to prevent the proliferation of priests, monks and churches. But Orthodoxy spread at the expense of Catholicism, chiefly through mixed marriages, and it is reported that towards the end of Venetian rule only two noble families adhered to the Latin faith. Toleration and assimilation were found on all levels and it was a natural result of the Venetian policy that on Corfu there was less rivalry than in most other places between the followers of the two faiths.

JEWS AND GYPSIES

Benjamin Tudela's twelfth-century account of the Jews in Greece records only one in Corfu. Under Angevin rule, however, a Jewish colony was encouraged and a ghetto, complete with synagogue, was established in the Campiello district of the town. By 1386 the strength of the community is illustrated by its representation of two in a Corfiote deputation of six that visited Venice. Around 1540 a second ghetto was established between the harbour and Voulgaris Street. This catered for refugees from the persecutions in Spain and Portugal and later for the Jews that fled from Naples, Apulia and Calabria. In 1665, according to Marmora, the Jewish community in Corfu numbered 500 houses.

Although less favourable than that of the Orthodox community, the position of the Corfiote Jew was much better than in other Venetian dominions. The Corfiote communities were alone exempted when Jews were banned from Venetian territories by the decree of 1572, and Venice insisted on their proper treatment. But the constant repetition of edicts indicates that the lot of the Jews was far from good, as does Marmora's comment that 'they would have been rich if they had been left alone'. The Jews were compelled to wear a yellow mark on the breast or hat as a badge of servitude, which an ordinance of 1532 explains was a 'substitute for the custom of stoning, which does so much injury to the houses'! Miller relates the absurd tales that were current about the Corfiote Jews. 'Travellers were told that one of them was a lineal descendant of Judas, and it was rumoured that a young Jewish girl was about to give birth to a Messiah.' The Jews were likely to be seized for the galleys or made to act as executioners with gallows erected in their cemetery. Yet in spite of abuse and degradation the Jewish community thrived. Towards the close of the Venetian period they had monopolised much of the trade as middle-men and the landed proprietors were in their debt, not only for money but also furniture, plate and livery.

The gypsies formed another interesting minority in Venetian Corfu. They are first mentioned during the Angevin period when their knowledge of horse-breeding gave them considerable prestige. The Venetians awarded the gypsies a special fief 'to reward public services', but what these services were remains conjecture. They were subject to the exclusive jurisdiction of the baron upon which their fief was bestowed, 'an office', states Marmora, 'of not a little gain and of very great honour'. Such a situation, however, proved advantageous and disadvantageous to the gypsy community. They were not compelled to serve in the galleys nor to render the usual feudal tributes of the other peasants, but being the exclusive property of the feudal lord the baron could inflict any punishment on them short of death – a 'privilege' denied to all his peers.

EDUCATION AND THE ARTS

The Venetian Republic did very little for Ionian education during the four centuries of its rule. The administration was content to pay only a few teachers of Greek and Italian and to grant young Ionian men the special privilege of taking a degree at the University of Padua. This was usually in law or medicine and without examination. Some private instruction was available and literacy could be gained from monastic teaching, but education was poorly developed and available to only a privileged minority. The historian Mario Pieri, a native of Corfu, remarked that towards the end of the eighteenth century there were no schools, no library, no printing press and no regular bookseller on the island. The only literature that could be bought was a Latin grammar and dictionary displayed in the shop-window of a chemist.

The initiative to improve intellectual life came from the Corfiotes themselves, although most of the developments in education and literature took place outside the island. In 1626 Thomas Flaginis founded a school and seminary in Venice where Greek boys from poor families could receive the benefits of an integrated Greek and Italian education. Flaginis, as a native of Corfu, followed the usual practice of his day by studying at Padua and subsequently a career as a lawyer in Venice. The Flaginian school produced a long line of teachers who served in provincial Greek schools and contributed to the Greek Enlightenment of the seventeenth and eighteenth centuries. The school is perhaps best remembered for an anthology of prose and poetry entitled *Flowers of Piety* and dedicated to the Assumption of the Virgin. Written by the pupils, it comprised epigrams in ancient Greek and Latin, Sapphic odes, Italian sonnets, and, most significantly, prose and verse compositions in demotic modern Greek. As such it offers the first surviving demotic poetry following the termination of the Cretan Renaissance by the Turkish capture of the island in 1669, and some of its pieces still find a place in the anthologies of modern Greek poetry. The estate of Thomas Flaginis was situated near the village of Anemomilós and efforts have been made to restore the ruined house as a historical monument.

Other Corfiotes, chiefly resident abroad, contributed to Greek intellectual development. Jacobo Triboles, a sixteenth-century resident of Venice, published in his native dialect a poem called 'History of the King of Scotland and the Queen of England'. Another literary Corfiote was Antonios Eparchos the author of a *Lament for the Fall of Greece*. Several Corfiote bards sang of the Venetian victories and in 1672 Andrea Marmora published in Italian the first history of Greece from earliest times to the loss of Crete by the Venetians. With the fall of Constantinople in 1453, Crete had become a refuge for scholars and artists from the mainland. Under Venetian rule the island kept its identity in language, religion, folklore and art and it became one of the last outposts of Orthodox Greek culture. When Crete fell to the Turks many Cretans fled to other parts of the Venetian empire. Venice in particular had a large Cretan colony, but others settled in Corfu and Zante where artists such as Moschos, Tzanes and Poulakis founded an original school of Ionian painting. It combined Cretan starkness with Baroque voluptuousness and culminated in the works of Doxaras, father and son.

These writers and artists in the Ionian Islands paved the way for the real intellectual renaissance which affected Corfu in the nineteenth century. Boulgaris and Theotokes played leading roles in the regeneration of Greek as a living literary language and were forerunners of the more celebrated Adamantios Korais. To the disgust of the clergy Boulgaris wrote in a language which the common people could understand!

THE TURKS AND THE DEFENCES

From the fourteenth century onwards the territorial expansion of the Turks formed the major threat to Greece. The Latin states fell one after another to Ottoman rule and with the capture of Constantinople in 1453 the Turks were in control of almost all the Greek mainland. The defence of the Greek littoral fell to the Venetians. The first Turko–Venetian war lasted from 1464 to 1479, and thereafter there was intermittent warfare which resulted in many changes in Venetian sovereignty. But not until the Duchy of Naxos and the island of Chios had fallen in 1566 did the Turks gain the major control of the Aegean. In 1648 the epic Siege of Candia (Iraklion) in Crete began and after twenty-two years this island also came under Turkish domination. During all these operations against the Turks the Corfiotes distinguished themselves in their active co-operation with Venice. There are references to Corfiotes fighting at Parga, Butrinto, Corinth, Patras and Lepanto, and the privilege of electing the captain of the Corfiote war-galleys was the reward of this loyalty.

The first Turko–Venetian confrontation over Corfu was accidental. In spring 1537 a large Ottoman fleet sailed near the island on its way to attack the Kingdom of Naples. The troop ships and those carrying weapons of war became entangled with Venetian galleys and hostilities broke out. Venice was ready to make amends for the incident but Suleiman the Magnificent resolved to avenge the insult to the Turkish flag. From Butrinto he despatched a large force under the command of Khair Eddin, 'Barbarossa', to take Corfu. The Turks landed at Govino, destroyed the village of Potamos and marched upon the town. The Corfiote forces consisted of 4,000 Italians and Greeks and to economise on provisions the garrison evicted the women, old men and children. These augmented the inhabitants who were refused admittance to the fort and the Corfiote traveller, Noukios, an eye-witness of the siege, left a graphic account of the sufferings of the islanders who begged for food at the Turkish lines or lay in the ditches to die. Provisions in the fort held out and when, after thirteen days, sickness broke out among the Turks the siege was lifted. But Corfu had been ravaged by fire and the sword and thousands of islanders were taken captive.

The Turkish invasion revealed the inadequacies of the Corfu defences. These were still confined to the Old Fort promontory, although the town had begun to spill out beyond what is now the Esplanade. The first peak had been fortified as early as 1149 when Byzantine and Venetian forces expelled the Norman garrison. In all probability the defences on the second peak were the work of the Venetians during their brief occupation of the island at the beginning of the thirteenth century. Following the siege of 1537 new bastions were erected and the citadel was separated from the town by a canal. When John Loche visited Corfu in 1553 the citadel had only just been 'trenched about with the sea and spanned by a drawbridge'. The materials for these defences came from the ancient city of Corcyra which the Corfiotes regarded as a handy quarry.

Yet Corfu's defences were still inadequate. Fresne-Canaye, who visited the island in 1572, admired the huge fortress and its 700 pieces of artillery which were said to have a firing-range reaching the Albanian coast. But he was astonished to learn that the Turks had been able to lay waste the island the previous year with 560 horsemen. The defence problem is apparent in a document of 1553 which is a report of a bailie to Venice on his appointment in Corfu. 'All the expense would be wasted', he maintained, 'if the defences of the old fortress were not brought up to date to withstand modern methods of siege and warfare.' In spite of the 200,000 ducat investment, the defences remained ineffective for 'the enemy without putting hand to sword could come and set his artillery right on the counterscarp'. Similar complaints flood from the pens of other Venetian officials and for much of the sixteenth century the Turks were free to plunder the Corfiote countryside.

The New Fort was built between 1570 and 1588. It was sited one kilometre from the Old Fort on a hill formerly called Saint Mark's and it dominated the harbour. The bastions were linked by a maze of galleries and underground communications and a line of further defences, consisting of scarps and fosses, extended from the New Fort to Garitsa Bay, thereby enclosing the town

(Fig 9). These were breached by three main gates; the Spilia Gate close to the harbour, the Royal Gate on the road to San Rocco and the Raimondo Gate where the road from the present Esplanade descends to the waterfront at Garitsa Bay. Further construction also continued on the Old Fort including the completion of two bastions which formed a defensive support for Mandraki. This was a small artificial military port where the Venetians could shelter ten galleys. The Old Fort also housed the palace, churches and private residences, and its barracks could shelter 12,000 men.

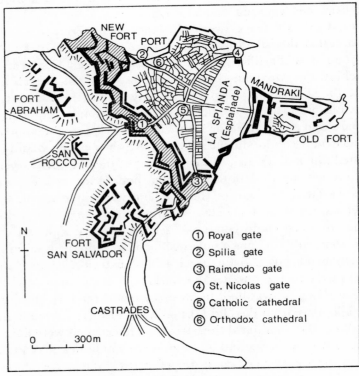

Fig 9   The later Venetian town and defences

THE SIEGE OF 1716

With the loss of Crete to the Turks, Corfu assumed increased importance to the Republic and during the Turko–Venetian war of 1684–99 it was used as winter quarters for the Venetian troops. Francesco Morosini, the hero of the Candian resistance, made it one of the bases for the Venetian recovery of the Peloponnesus, but this was short-lived and by the turn of the century the Ottoman reconquest of southern Greece was rapid. Cythera and Lefkas were abandoned without struggle and the Venetians fell back on Corfu. The celebrated siege of Corfu in 1716 was the last struggle between Venice and the Turks and the last great attempt by the Turks to extend their conquests in Christendom.

The Venetians engaged Count John Matthias von der Schulenburg to defend the island. He was a soldier of fortune who had fought with distinction under the Duke of Marlborough at the Siege of Tournai and the Battle of Malplaquet. Armed with the rank of field-marshal he arrived in Corfu with foreign regiments hired for its defence. The Turks disembarked 30,000 men and their first objectives were the hills of Mount Abraham and San Salvatore to the west of the town. The entire urban population was armed, but Schulenburg wrote that he was 'in want of everything' and his motley garrison of Germans, Italians, Slavs and Greeks numbered only 8,000. Even the women and priests were armed 'and one monk', according to Miller, 'with a huge iron crucifix in his hands, was a conspicuous figure as he charged the besiegers, invoking vengeance of God upon their heads'.

The siege lasted forty-two days. On 17–18 August the Turkish assault had forced the defenders back to the Old Fort, only to be driven out of the town by Schulenburg heading a party of 800 men. The Corfiotes awaited a renewed assault, but it never came. On the night of 18 August one of Corfu's freak thunderstorms appears to have demoralised the Turkish army

81

which had also received news of the total defeat of the sultan's army at Peterwardein by Prince Eugene of Austria. During the following night the whole Turkish force sailed secretly away leaving behind their guns and barrage-trains. According to popular belief the panic-stricken Turks saw a number of acolytes carrying lighted candles, and an aged bishop pursuing the infidels staff in hand. The bishop was identified with Saint Spiridon, the island's patron, and the Corfiotes will never accept any other explanation for the Turkish defeat!

The Republic granted Marshal Schulenburg an annuity of 5,000 ducats for life, presented him with a jewelled sword and erected a statue to him at the Old Fort. Schulenburg was awarded the rare privilege of having his effigy erected during his lifetime and in the inscription he is termed the general-in-chief, not of Venice, but of the Christian commonwealth. Under Schulenburg's directions Corfu's final fortifications were erected. These consisted of strong defences on Mount Abraham and San Salvatore which were linked with underground passages.

VENICE IN DECLINE

The Turkish wars practically ended the Venetian Republic's tenure as an eastern Mediterranean power. From its once-vast Levantine possessions, only the Ionian Islands and their dependencies remained under the Venetian flag and even these were preserved more by the decadence of the Turks than by the strength of the Republic. On Corfu the Venetians maintained an outward show of pomp but the administrative officials sent from the capital were inferior and arrived intent to make fortunes by extorting as much as possible from the local population. Decadence and corruption reached its zenith on Zakinthos, but heavy taxation, oppressive laws and fraud were equally prevalent on Corfu. The *provveditore-generale* lived on a grand scale and his lesser officials flourished on blackmail and anonymous denunciations. The desire for luxuries continued to actuate life in the town, but the countryside had fallen into a deplorable state of poverty. Few proprietors had the capital to invest in improvements and the lack of beasts of burden and carriageable roads produced immense difficulties. Visitors to the island regarded the rural population as ignorant, poor and indolent.

Corfu remained the centre of the Republic's naval force, but this too had fallen into decline through bad discipline. Attacks by Barbary corsairs considerably inconvenienced the islanders and Venice was forced to appoint Angelo Emo as 'an extraordinary captain of the ships'. Following his reorganisation of the navy he succeeded in curtailing Algerian and Tunisian piracy and his name came to rank with those of Morosini and Schulenburg in the Venetian history of western Greece.

The French Revolution had little immediate impact on the islands, although there were some disturbances on Zakinthos, and on Corfu the islanders were growing restless with the exclusive privileges of the nobles. A special commissioner was despatched from Venice to reform the constitution of the islands but this merely achieved a reduction in the number of council members at Corfu and Lefkas. Greater hopes were raised in 1794 with the arrival of Widmann, the last Venetian *provveditore-generale*. Widmann's successful administrative career in the navy, his dislike for ceremony and his well-known benevolence, convinced the Corfiotes that a real attempt would be made to end corruption.

Widmann found a depleted Ionian treasury and after pledging his own fortune to meet the pressing needs of the administration, he appealed to the islanders for funds to carry on the government. The Jews contributed substantial sums of money and also armed a number of soldiers at their own expense. Yet the economic and military position of the Ionian Islands remained weak and it was reported that the fortifications on Corfu contained scarcely enough powder for a single man-of-war. Venice could provide little practical assistance for the days of La Serenissma were rapidly drawing to a close.

6   RUSSIAN AND FRENCH INTERLUDES

WITH the declining political and commercial prestige of the Venetian Republic the strategic values of Corfu and the Ionian Islands assumed increasing importance. Towards the end of the eighteenth century many nations looked on them with envy and some, notably France, Russia, the Ottoman empire and Britain, translated this envy into possession. After 1788 Russian and French rivalry in the southern Balkans was turned into a triangular power-conflict when Ali Pasha became Governor of Epirus and gradually created a virtually independent state in defiance to the Sultan of Constantinople. Russian agents, based on the consulate at Patras, were already active in the Peloponnesus and the French were quick to establish diplomatic arrangements with Ioannina, the Epirot capital.

Ali Pasha was of Albanian birth and he made Ioannina the most influential and, in a curious way, the most civilised capital in the southern Balkans. He was an able but ruthless tyrant who 'had no scruples', states Woodhouse, 'in playing off the rival contenders against each other and he never kept his word for longer than it suited him to do so'. He ignored the Ottoman sultan, executed his emissaries and treated all his rivals with impartial treachery. Ali Pasha's major ambitions were to crush the independent Greek mainland community of Souli, against which he had waged a series of wars in the closing years of the eighteenth century, and then to acquire the Ionian Islands and their Epirot dependencies. Thus the expansionist ambitions of Napoleon Bonaparte proved to be in direct conflict with those of Ali Pasha.

84

THE FIRST FRENCH PERIOD

In May 1797 following a series of brilliant victories in northern Italy, Bonaparte's army entered Venice and abolished the oligarchic republic. Under the Treaty of Campo Formio the Venetian possessions were divided between France and Austria, with the former gaining the Ionian Islands and their mainland dependencies. In the August prior to the Treaty, Bonaparte had written to the Directory stating that 'Corfu, Zante and Cefalonia are of more interest to us than the whole of Italy' and to Talleyrand he stressed that 'Corfu and Zante make us masters of the Adriatic and the Levant'. 'It is useless', he continued, 'to try to maintain the Turkish empire; we shall see its downfall in our lifetime. The occupation of the Ionian Islands will put us in a position to support it or to secure a share of it ourselves.' Bonaparte viewed the islands as a springboard to the East and the strategic importance of Corfu in particular was proportionally increased at a time when the Ottoman empire was in decline. 'The greatest misfortune that could happen to me', he said, 'would be the loss of Corfu.'

The French as well as the British feared the Russian occupation of the islands as a fulfilment of their long-desired goal for a base in the Mediterranean. In the guise of an ally of Venice and with Venetian forces mixing with his own, the French General Gentilly sailed into Corfu on 11 July. Bonaparte's military deception and cunning is revealed in his instructions to Gentilly who was to show outward respect to the authority of Venice. 'If the inhabitants should prove to be inclined towards independence (that is to say, inclined to free themselves from Venetian rule), you are to encourage that inclination, and in the proclamation you will be issuing you must not omit to speak of Greece, Sparta and Athens.' Gentilly delivered his speech in French, Italian and Greek and informed the Corfiotes that the French Republic, in alliance with the Venetians, would revive the glories and virtues of classical Greece in the

Ionian Islands. An enthusiastic reception was given to the French command and Bonaparte wrote of it to the Directory:

> An immense crowd were on the seafront to welcome our troops with cries of happiness and enthusiasm, now that they had gained their liberty. At the head of the crowds was the Papa, or the chief priest of the religion of the country, a learned man already advanced in years. He approached General Gentilly and said: 'Frenchman, you will find in this island a people ignorant of those sciences and arts which make nations distinguished, but do not despise them for that reason. They are capable of becoming again what they once were. Learn to appreciate their worth by reading this book.

The book proved to be Homer's *Odyssey*. Similar receptions were reported in Zakinthos, Lefkas and Cefalonia, but it appears that Bonaparte's letters to the Directory were more expressive of his own elation for the new territorial conquests than that of the islanders for their French rulers. At Passeriano on 13 September he wrote to the Minister of Exterior Relations: 'It appears to me that the grand maxim of the Republic ought henceforth to be never to abandon Corfu, Zante etc: we should find resources for our commerce which would be of great moment to us and to the future course of events in Europe . . . With the island of San Pietro, which has been ceded to us by the King of Sardinia, joined to Malta and Corfu, we shall be masters of all the Mediterranean.' A request to the Directory led to reinforcement troops arriving in Corfu under the command of General Chabot.

The French undermined the *ancien régime* by introducing sweeping reforms in their customary manner. They burned the Golden Book, decreed the abolition of feudalism, reorganised civil and criminal justice, extended education facilities and democratised government. The islands were organised into the three *départements* of Corfu, Ithaca and the Aegean Sea (Zante, Strophades, Cythera and Anticythera) and each was to be represented in Paris by an elected deputy. Count Andreas Sordinas became the deputy of the Corfu *département* which also included the islands of Paxos, Antipaxos, Fano and Merlero and the mainland areas of Butrinto and Parga. Count Spiridon Theotokis was elected president of the reconstituted town council.

In spite of French Republican zeal Corfiote life was not greatly altered during the first French period and the aristocracy maintained their grip on society. The islanders had hoped that the French would relieve the heavy burden of taxation, but in fact the new administration was as penniless as its predecessor's and equally anxious to raise money. French popularity quickly declined and their mockery of the Orthodox Church also engendered contempt. The decision to grant Jews a civic status equal to the Orthodox Christians caused further discontent as did the suspected alliance of the French with Ali Pasha, the island's nearest Moslem enemy.

THE RUSSO–TURKISH ALLIANCE

The initial French occupation of the Ionian Islands was of short duration. Bonaparte's invasion of Egypt in 1789 involved him in war with Britain and the French defeat at the Battle of the Nile (1 August) by a fleet commanded by Nelson ultimately led to the loss of the Ionian Islands. On 1 September Turkey and Russia formed an unnatural coalition declaring war on the French Republic and ordering that all Frenchmen found in Turkish dominions should 'be seized as enemies of God, and men without faith and law'. General Chabot was unable to obtain either reinforcements or provisions for Corfu and his position was made critical by the aspirations of Ali Pasha. The French general had received specific instructions to encourage Ali Pasha in his endeavours to become independent of the Porte and as long as the French power was in the ascendant Ali Pasha made great protestations of friendship. When news reached him of the French defeat in Egypt he demanded from Chabot the dependencies of Butrinto, Parga, Prevenza, Vonitza and the fort of Lefkas. However, the appearance of a combined Russian and Turkish fleet off Cythera on 6 October provided Ali Pasha with the opportunity of taking the mainland dependencies.

The Russo–Turkish force under Vice-Admiral Ousakov and Abdel-kadir Bey moved northwards through the islands and once again conquerors were greeted as liberators. Only on Corfu did the French have sufficient strength to put up a fight, but Chabot was also faced with insurrection among the islanders who raised the standard of revolt in the suburb of Mantouki. It took 800 of Chabot's men and three gun-boats to drive the Corfiotes from their position on the heights opposite Fort Abraham and the battle lasted seven hours. On 5 November the Russo–Turkish fleet anchored off the island of Vido and demanded the surrender of the citadel and town in the names of the tsar and the sultan. The French garrison numbered 1,800 men, but the promised assistance of 3,000 men from Ancona determined Chabot to put up a spirited defence.

The siege lasted for several months and British aid to the Russo–Turkish cause came in the form of the eighteen-gun brig *El Corso,* commanded by Lord William Stuart. Nelson had repeatedly advised Ousakov to take a more extended view of the operations for he believed that Corfu would fall by itself once the French were driven from their more important positions in Italy and Egypt. The British assistance in the capture of Corfu was in fact an inducement to the Russian and Turkish admirals to send some of their forces to Messina. A depleted garrison and a lack of munitions and provisions led to Corfu's surrender in February 1799. The Russians occupied the old and new forts and the outworks were garrisoned by the Turks. To their disappointment the 12,000 Albanian auxiliaries were denied their promised reward for assistance, which was to have been twenty-four hours pillage of the town. Towards the end of March the French embarked for Ancona.

THE SEPTINSULAR REPUBLIC

Under a treaty signed in Constantinople in March 1800 the

Plate 17 (right) 'The Dying Achilles' in the ornamental gardens of the Achilleon Palace

Plate 18 (below) Renovation work at the Palaeokastritsa monastery

Plate 19 (left) A fruit and vegetable stall well-stocked with the rich produce of the island

Plate 20 (below) The arcaded Liston, the town's main social and entertainment centre

Ionian Islands became known as the Septinsular or Heptanesian Republic, the first independent Greek state of modern times. With its capital at Corfu and its own flag, the state had the right to establish diplomatic relations but it remained subject to Turkish suzerainty, and Russian forces remained in occupation for the islands' protection, without which they might well have been seized by Ali Pasha. From the day of its foundation, however, the Septinsular Republic developed administrative problems and a number of constitutions and methods of government were formulated during its two-year existence. Initially a scheme of federation was tried and a senate, whose president was styled *archon*, met at Corfu and a local council of nobles sat in each island. The constitution of 1801 proclaimed freedom of rights, universal suffrage and democratic rule, but a more conservative constitution was adopted in 1803 which limited participation and representation in government to a small percentage of the population. In effect the oligarchical features of the Venetian régime were revived, with the difference that privilege was now based on property rather than on birth qualifications. The prerequisites for nobility were:

> To have been born of legitimate marriage of Christian parents in one of the seven islands; to possess an annual revenue at Corfu of 1,800 ducats, Cefalonia 675, Zante 1,350, Lefkas 540, Cythera 255, Ithaca 315, Paxos 54; not to exercise any mechanical or other art; not to keep a shop; to have always a decent life, and to be able to read and write in one of the languages used by the government; never to have been found guilty of infamous crimes of fraudulency.

It is noteworthy that the Corfiote Count John Capodistrias, who later won fame as foreign minister of Russia and president of the Greek state, played a prominent role in the drafting of this constitution. However, the régime was thoroughly reactionary and aristocratic and there were uprisings throughout the islands. As secretary of the Septinsular government, Capodistrias introduced a series of constitutional changes in an attempt to satisfy opposing factions but the system led to

F

separation. Cefalonia and Ithaca proclaimed their independence and Zante hoisted the British flag. At a National Assembly held in Corfu the islands were charged with rebellion and treason and were left to their own devices. Even in Corfu the struggle between the upper and middle classes was severe and it was reported that 'anarchy stalked about like a local phantom, spreading desolation and ruin'. Organised violence spread throughout the island and assassins carried their attacks to the gates of the city.

In an attempt to restore law and order a Corfiote deputation was sent to St Petersburg to request a new government from Tsar Alexander and armed forces to support its working. Count Mocenigo, a Zantiote nobleman who had risen to the position of Russian plenipotentiary, was sent to Corfu with full powers of government. Order and tranquillity were restored but Mocenigo was accused of amassing a considerable private fortune by following the example of the Venetian *provveditores*. He was further criticised for his extravagant military and civil expenditure.

THE SECOND FRENCH PERIOD

In 1803 war again broke out between France and Britain, but it seemed at first that the great powers would respect the independence of the Septinsular Republic. Russia, however, soon lost sight of its pledge to the islands, and Bonaparte, now elevated to the status of emperor, had not forgotten the strategic advantage of Corfu – advantage which had increased in importance since the British occupation of Malta. Russia was the only European power with the capacity to resist French expansion and Bonaparte was anxious for the reversal of alliances. The Treaties of Tilsit (8 July 1807) signed between himself and Tsar Alexander reconciled France and Russia and included schemes for the partition of the Turkish empire in Europe. As part of the agreements Russia ceded its rights over the Ionian Islands and Bonaparte interpreted this as complete suzerainty to France. He ordered General Berthier to sail for the islands and to fortify Corfu strongly – 'la clef de l'Adriatique'. The French garrison numbered some 20,000 men.

Once secured, General François Donzelot was appointed commandant for the islands. It appears that he was a man of talent, integrity and exceptional charm who, according to Kirkwall, 'was the most popular ruler who ever landed in the Seven Islands'. Accustomed to strict military discipline from active service in Russia and Prussia, Donzelot administered the islands with severity but fairness. This task was made easier by the policies of Bonaparte who, with usual sagacity and perceiving the weakpoints of the islanders, made Greek Orthodoxy the official religion and resurrected the Golden Book. The former declaration pleased the country-people and the latter played to the Signori by nominally recognising their powers in the courts of justice and the senate. The French conciliatory policy reaped its own rewards for when the southern islands received the British troops with open arms the Corfiotes, accepting Donzelot as a man of ability, remained loyal to France.

Although the second French period was again of short duration (1807–14), it made a significant impact on the life of Corfu. The French appreciated both the beauty of the island and the character of the Corfiotes, particularly their hospitality. The large French garrison contributed substantially to local commerce as well as to the animation of the town. Relationships between the troops and the islanders were friendly and correct. Letters written to France comment on the social life which included the theatre, balls and numerous cultural events. Graphic accounts are also given of the more traditional aspects of Corfiote life, including the rich local costumes and village pageants. Many marriages took place between the troops and Corfiote girls and the romantic French were eager to relate the amours of their commanding officers.

The creation of the Ionian Society in 1808 was the idea of Donzelot who was keen to foster science and the arts, agriculture, commerce and industry, and to encourage local crafts.

Architecturally the major achievement of the French was the celebrated arcaded buildings bordering the town's Esplanade. They consist of two handsome rows of houses which became known as the Liston from the 'list' of families entitled to walk and sit under its arcades. The style resembles that of the Rue de Rivoli in Paris and must have provided a nostalgic reminder of the delights of the French capital. The horse-drawn landaus, still in use in the town today, offered further Parisian flavour.

THE FALL OF THE FRENCH

The setback to British *amour propre* in the Mediterranean by the French occupation of the Ionian Islands was intensified by the loss of Capri to the French in 1808. In 1809 Vice-Admiral Lord Collingwood learned from a deputation of Cefalonian and Zantiote merchants that they were eager to regain their independence and a strong British force sailing under sealed orders from Sicily had no difficulty in occupying the southern islands. It appeared that the British intention was merely to liberate the islands from French rule, but the instructions given by Collingwood to Captain Spranger were indicative of wider British aspirations. Once the French were expelled the islands were to garrison themselves but in consideration of the assistance given by Britain the ministers appointed for the administration and government were to be recognised and approved by the British commanders. A British officer was also appointed to each island to head the government and although a council was formed to carry out civil matters the British commander was omnipotent.

Corfu was no longer the dilapidated fortress which General Chabot had vainly endeavoured to defend. With an army of 40,000–50,000 men and 500 new pieces of artillery, it was considered too strong to be attacked. The island of Vido, denuded of its olive trees and strengthened by fieldworks, protected the sea approaches to the town. Britain attempted to blockade the island with two frigates which in the view of William Turner 'was the most imperfect act of hostility ever enforced. Telegraphs are established all along the coasts of the island, and as soon as these report the two frigates . . . to be out of sight, boats immediately run over to the coast of Albania and bring back plentiful supplies of corn and cattle.' Ali Pasha respected the power of the French and although he asked a high price for his supplies he was not in a position to refuse them.

The stalemate lasted until the middle of February 1814 when a detachment of British troops under Colonel Church took Paxos as a preliminary to an attack on Corfu. But the British forces in the islands were small and the capture of Paxos was a feint which neither intimidated nor impressed Donzelot. Bonaparte's abdication superseded Donzelot's preparations for war and on official orders from Louis XVIII Corfu was surrendered to General James Campbell who accepted it in the name of the allies.

The question of the disposal of the islands attracted the attention of the major powers of the time. At the Congress of Vienna – the international assembly convened to determine the settlement of Europe after the Napoleonic Wars – the British representative proposed that the Seven Islands should pass under the complete sovereignty of George III. Count John Capodistrias, the Russian plenipotentiary and himself a Corfiote, insisted on the freedom of the islands and was willing to cede no more than a protectorate over them to Britain. In the final arrangements, signed in Paris in 1815, the islands became such a protectorate under the title of the United States of the Ionian Islands. They were to be governed by a British Lord High Commissioner from whom they were to receive a constitution. In the interim, however, they were included in the governorship of Malta.

The British occupation of the islands dashed the hopes of patriotic Greeks that the islands would play an immediate and major role in the Greek struggle for independence against Turkish rule. But Capodistrias took a longer view and believed that the Ionians, who had been spared the long years of

Turkish occupation, were well suited to become the leaven of an independent Greece. The French domination of Europe was over and this had been the greatest obstacle to the regeneration of Greece.

7   ALL THINGS BRIGHT AND BRITISH

THE former High Commissioner's Palace, and subsequently that of the Greek royal family, is the most impressive monument to British rule in Corfu. It stands on the northern side of the Esplanade. This large Regency neo-classical building is constructed of white Maltese stone and has an elegant Doric portico which projects on either side to form a curving screen pierced with triumphal arches and terminating in balanced pavilions. Above the two tiers of Georgian windows is a decoration in relief of medallions representing the emblems of the Ionian Islands: Cephalus the hunter for Cefalonia; Zakinthos seated with lance in hand for Zante; the head of Odysseus for Ithaca; Bellerophon on Pegasus for Lefkas; a trident for Paxos; Aphrodite and a dolphin for Cythera; and a rudderless ship for Corfu – a symbol of the island's independent spirit. The focal point of the skyline, now removed, was Britannia seated in a barque.

The palace, dedicated to St Michael and St George, was built between 1818 and 1823 after plans of Colonel (later General Sir George) Whitmore. It is the oldest official building in Greece and as many would argue the finest non-ecclesiastical building to be erected since antiquity. Originally the palace provided a home and residence for the British High Commissioners, a seat for the Ionian Senate, and the headquarters and treasury for the Order of Saints Michael and George, instituted by the Prince Regent in 1818 to reward services in Malta and the Ionian Islands. The two archways which flank the main façade are respectively labelled the

97

Gate of the Archangel Michael and the Gate of Saint George.

In his unpublished memoirs, recently unearthed by Stelio Hourmouzios, Whitmore describes his difficulties with the plans and construction for it was only after his design was accepted that he was told the legislative chambers were to be housed in the same building. All three functions are apparent in the architecture and decoration of the palace which was officially opened on St George's Day, 1823. The state rooms (throne-room, ballroom and dining-room) were planned on a scale befitting their purpose and their ornamentation was executed with Adam-like care. They expressed the pomp and circumstance of the British government and during official functions they were filled with Ionian senators wearing the star and mantle of the Order. They were complemented by officers from the garrison and the High Commissioner's staff dressed in the ceremonial uniforms of the period.

In 1864 the palace was given to George I, King of the Hellenes, and it served as a royal residence until 1913. During World War I and the Metaxas dictatorship it fell into disrepair but escaped damage in the bombardment of Corfu in World War II. For a period it was used as a temporary billet for Greek refugees during the civil war and both its external and internal fabric remained in a dilapidated condition. A private trust for its renovation was established in 1954 by Sir Charles Peake, then British Ambassador in Athens. The state rooms were restored to their original splendour by the Corfiote architect John Kollas and several of the former residential apartments now house archaeological items and *objects d'art* bequeathed by private donors. The interior is frowned upon by the busts and portraits of the self-assured High Commissioners whose monuments are further scattered throughout the town.

The palace is described by Nigel Nicolson in Sacheverell Sitwell's *Great Palaces*. He states, that it is included not because it is a great palace in the formal sense but because of its unusual origins and associations and the manner in which it blends British and Hellenic traditions. 'It stands, faintly mottled by time and tribulation, . . . as much loved by Corfiotes . . . as if it has been erected by Greeks for Greeks, instead of by a frustrated Colonel of Engineers for the rather surly representatives of foreign power.'

SIR THOMAS MAITLAND

The British Protectorate of the Ionian Islands has been described as one of the oddest, often most comical, conjunctions in modern history. To a large extent this was the result of the colourful, generally eccentric, characters of the Lord High Commissioners in whose hands all executive power was vested. In 1816 Sir Thomas Maitland, former Governor of Malta, was appointed as the first High Commissioner. The wisdom of this choice has often been questioned for at best Maitland was a benevolent autocrat whose personal habits and public etiquette came under constant criticism. 'If able and honest,' states William Miller, 'Maitland was a rough soldier, who looked like a bulldog, whose language surprised the elegant Ionians by its coarseness and whose convivial habits disgusted a naturally abstemious people.' James Napier, who served under Maitland, described him as 'insufferably rude and abrupt . . . dirty in his person and constantly drunk and surrounded by sycophants'. Maitland was particularly adverse to bearers of letters of introduction to whom, on one occasion, he exposed his behind! Another incident relates his appearance in the senate room clothed in a shirt, a red night-cap and a pair of slippers. Napier's *The Colonies*, published in 1833, records further illustrations of Maitland's boorishness but acknowledges the shrewd Scotsman as a man of considerable talents. 'His rule', he states, 'was sagacious and on the whole beneficial', and Maitland 'introduced many much-needed reforms'.

On his arrival in Corfu Maitland found a peasantry ground down by the usurious loans of their landlords, an empty treasury, and judges that were openly bribed. His first task was the formulation of a new constitutional charter but one which kept the executive power firmly in his hands. Maitland considered the islanders as unfit for a true form of parliamentary democracy and from his dictatorial powers he acquired the nickname 'King Tom'.

The Ionian constitution of 2 May 1817 created a bicameral legislative consisting of an Assembly of forty members and a Senate of six members. The Assembly's official term of office was five years and it met biennially in Corfu for not more than thirty days. The Senate was headed by a president, appointed by the British sovereign on the recommendation of the High Commissioner. He was drawn from the ranks of the Ionian nobles, bore the title 'Highness', and was received with full military honours. The president was the most important person in the Ionian State after the High Commissioner, on whose favour he depended for nomination and the renewal of his appointment. The first president was Baron Emmanual Theotokis, a member of a famous Corfiote family and a firm friend of Britain. The representatives of the other islands were again vetoed by the High Commissioner. They took rank immediately from him and were given the title 'Residents'. On Corfu the High Commissioner was the island's Resident. The Senate was responsible for the appointment of Regents as heads of local municipal councils, but since every Regent required the approval of the Resident, who in turn was appointed by the High Commissioner, the power of the latter throughout the protectorate was omnipotent. The High Commissioner also sanctioned the two Ionian members of the Supreme Council of Justice who held office with two British judges nominated by the sovereign.

Maitland's constitution provided a deceptive but false appearance of parliamentary government and was not appreciably altered until 1848. The Legislative Assembly had little real power for its short biennial meetings meant that business was frequently left unfinished and much time was wasted picking up the threads from previous sessions. There was little opportunity for public criticism of the system for printing-presses could not be erected without the consent of the High Commissioner. The official *Gazette of the United States of the Ionian Islands*, first published at Zakinthos under a different title in 1810 and subsequently transferred to Corfu, was for long the sole Ionian newspaper and it was originally published in Italian. Greek was declared the official idiom, but English was used by the police, maintenance and postal departments. Italian was used in the legislature until 1849 and only in 1852 was Greek made obligatory in public offices.

Illiberal as Maitland's constitution now appears, it was characteristic of the age and must be judged by its results. Its purpose was to elevate the conditions of the lower classes and curb the greed and power of the ruling families. By a number of fiscal measures the peasantry were released from the financial bondage of the nobles and the latter no longer controlled the courts of justice. The rural communities also benefited from the construction of roads and other public works, and trade and agriculture were encouraged. The result of Maitland's work was an era of peace and prosperity unparalleled on the Greek mainland, and the sound economic base was an encouragement to cultural and intellectual life.

Maitland's other concern was to foster the loyalty of influential Ionians to the British crown and a sound way of achieving this was the creation of an order of knighthood which bestowed high-sounding epithets on senators and deputies. This gratified the Greek love of titles, and the nobility, especially at the seat of government in Corfu, became the strongest supporters of British rule. The Order of St Michael and St George provided a means of conferring a mark of royal favour on both natives of the Ionian Islands and Malta. True to character, Maitland himself was the first Grand Master of the new order and plans were set in motion for the building of the palace in which the investitures were carried out. 'The crafty old man', wrote Napier, 'laughed in his sleeve when he opened ostentatiously the Halls of St Michael and St George and saw all the Corfu galaxy in their brilliant decorations of chivalry.' His amusement was undoubtedly heightened by the design of the 'Ionian uniform' which included a pair of bright-yellow breeches!

Maitland died of apoplexy on an official visit to Malta in 1824. His memorial in Corfu is an Ionian Rotunda erected on the southern side of the Esplanade. The proportions of the edifice are a fitting tribute to his autocratic rule, but Sheldon is perhaps a little harsh when he suggests it was built as the 'abortion' of his exceptional ugliness.

SIR FREDERICK ADAM

Although not without grave faults Maitland's constitution worked well when properly administered. Subsequent High Commissioners, however, many with little governmental experience, were careless in the application of Maitland's reforms which ultimately led to revolutionary fever in 1848. Sir Frederick Adam governed the islands from 1824 to 1832. He was another Scot with a distinguished army record, but unlike Maitland he was a cultivated, vain and easily flattered man who enjoyed grand living and consumed his time on petty pompous ceremonies. Preoccupation with high society and lavish entertaining led to his neglect of the lower classes and a lukewarm enforcement of the reforms instituted to control the activities of the nobility.

Publically and privately the lives of Sir Frederick and Lady Adam are graphically revealed in the Letters of Private Wheeler, a member of the Corfiote garrison, and in the violent tirade against Adam written by Colonel Napier, Resident of Cefalonia. According to the latter, Adam was caught in a compromising situation with a Corfiote lady: a divorce ensued and the lady, Nina Palatianou, became Lady Adam, whose lovers were said to rival the number of public works she instigated. Most of her portraits reveal extensive depilatory treatment for according to Wheeler, 'like most Greek women she had something interesting about her, but the beard on her upper lip would ornament an hussar'. Despite this defect Sir Frederick was in love with Nina and Corfu and almost all the revenue of the Ionian Islands was spent on the two. Nina's expensive tastes matched her ambitions and she persuaded her husband to build the large villa of Mon Repos barely 2 miles from the official palace. Napier's estimate of its cost between 1828 and 1831 was £20,000 – although like many of his statements this is an exaggeration and £8,000 was the realistic figure to the Ionian State. 'Sir Frederick's folly', as it came to be known, remained a royal residence until the Greek junta coup of 1967.

Further examples of Adam's extravagances were the purchases of a gold coat and a glass coach at the cost of £300 and £800 respectively. These were reserved for state occasions, but it appears the coat was ruined by a Corfiote downpour on the occasion of its first public appearance. The islanders affirmed that 'Corfu kept the Lord High Commissioner, Cefalonia paid his tailor, and Zakinthos his coach-maker'. To the Greeks, however, with their love of show and ceremony, Adam was perhaps the most popular of all the High Commissioners.

Extravagances aside, Adam's greatest benefit to Corfu was the construction of a great aqueduct which brought a permanent water-supply to the city from Benitses, 12km to the south. Prior to this water had been brought by pack animals a distance of 5km from the Potamos river to the north. He also carried out further improvements to communications and the road from Corfu to Palaeokastritsa was completed in 1828 by the British 11th Regiment Royal Engineers. The ample funds inherited from Maitland's government were soon depleted and not daring to borrow from the public treasury yet wanting to construct a road to the scenic area of Palaeokastritsa, Adam established a convalescent hospital there for British soldiers. This forced the hand of the Assembly to provide the necessary finance.

A large proportion of Adam's money came from the currant-producing islands of Cefalonia, Ithaca and Zante. These had benefited from the destruction of the currant-fields in the Peloponnesus during the early years of the Greek War of

Independence. Rightly they complained that Corfu was being enriched at their expense and Cefalonia under the Residency of Napier was the most restive. Napier proposed that the Ionian capital should be transferred from Corfu to Argostoli and ultimately his outspoken views and arbitrary methods led to his dismissal. His revenge was a bitter attack on Adam's inefficient government which on his departure from Corfu in 1832 left the administration in debt.

THE IONIAN ACADEMY

During their stay in Corfu Sir Frederick and Lady Adam were at the centre of a brilliant Anglo-Ionian circle which culminated in an intellectual and cultural renaissance in Corfu and the islands. Earlier the French had attempted to cultivate academic interests by the creation of the Ionian Society but this was disbanded with the end of French rule. In 1824 Lord Guilford founded the Ionian Academy and it was Corfu rather than Athens that developed as the principal Greek literary and intellectual centre of the nineteenth century.

Guilford was an ardent philhellene who devoted his fortune to the development of a Hellenic university. Napier regarded him as a 'pleasant' but 'queer fish' who 'goes about dressed up like Plato, with a gold band round his mad pate and flowering drapery of purple hue'. Guilford's headband was embroidered with olives and the owl of Athens and his classical attire was completed with an ancient-style mantle tied round his shoulders with a gold clasp. Another contemporary writer described 'the pretty dress of the students, consisting of a tunic and *chlamys* [cloak] with buskins of red leather reaching the mid-leg'. The professors bound fillets round their heads and the faculties were distinguished by the colour of their garments. 'Medicine had the tunic citron and the *chlamys* orange; law light green and violet; philosophy green and blue.' Whether Guilford was insane or merely eccentric will long be argued. His countrymen thought that he carried his colourful concern for the academy to the point of absurdity and his proposal to establish a Chair of Sanskrit was understandably met with little enthusiasm! Napier describes the babble and confusion of tongues which made up the academy. 'All the Greeks would speak Italian, the Italians English, the English French and Italian, and the French all the languages together.' Guilford would address 'every person in a different language, and always in that which the person addressed did not understand'!

Guilford's academy was initially housed in the vacated palace of the Venetian *Provveditore Generale* and in spite of its idiosyncrasies it attracted scholars from all over Greece. The library was furnished with some 25,000 books from Guilford's own collection and from donations and bequests of well-wishers. A steady stream of books became available in Modern Greek and the academy developed as a clearing-house for Ionian writers and the seat of a remarkable literary movement which prepared the artistic awakening of Greece.

Guilford died in England in 1827 after a short and unexpected illness and consequently many of his flamboyant and grandiose plans collapsed. The solicitor acting on behalf of his son, Lord Sheffield, requested the return of Guilford's books and manuscripts to London, but a clause in Guilford's will stated that his possessions were to become the property of the academy on condition that the Ionian government endowed it with an annual sum of £3,500. The clause was ignored and much of the library returned to England but it survived in part until 1943 when it was destroyed in the fighting between Italians and Germans. In 1837 the academy moved from its site in the Old Fort to one on the southern end of the Esplanade. In 1847 Sir George Brown, soon after leaving Oxford, became its rector. Increasingly, however, the academy was losing students to Pisa and Padua and other Italian centres of learning, as well as to the University of Athens which was founded in 1837. By 1863 the numbers of students in each faculty rarely exceeded twenty and shortly afterwards its departments were closed and merged with those of the University of Athens.

Guilford's monument in Corfu is a marble bust by Prosa-lendis, the founder of the School of Fine Arts. It stands in a small garden off the Esplanade along with other Corfiote notables. Perhaps his greatest monument is the obituary that appeared in the *Ionian Official Gazette* of 3 November 1827: 'Letters have lost in him one of their most powerful protectors, England one of her most erudite peers, society one of its most beneficient and honourable members, the youth of Greece its most loving father and benefactor.' Greece's indebtedness to Guilford is made clear by Vretos. 'What would have been the condition of learning in Greece', he wrote, 'if there had been no Earl of Guilford, and if he had not founded a university in Corfu which gave instruction to nearly all the doctors, lawyers, professors, teachers and civil functionaries of the present kingdom.'

POETS AND WRITERS

A host of poets, prose-writers, critics and historians are re-presentative of the creative abilities evident in the Ionian Islands during the first half of the nineteenth century. To a large extent, however, the leaders of the literary and intellectual movement were Dionysius Solomos (1798–1857) and Andreas Kalvos (1792–1869) who provided the essential direction to Greek poetry, setting its course and to a considerable degree determining its character. Solomos, who came to Corfu from Zakinthos in 1828, was a protégé of Sir Frederick and Lady Adam, and he is regarded, both in quality and in time, as the first poet of modern Greece. Educated in Venice and later at the University of Padua his first literary language, and that of his early poems, was Italian, but he began writing in Greek and elevated the demotic tongue to a refined artistic medium. Like Wordsworth he believed that the purest poetry was written in the simplest language and his use of demotic Greek expressed powerfully his feelings for nature, freedom, truth, love and death. Solomos drew both from the rich tradition of Greek folk poetry and from the cultivated poetry of Crete. His principal

works include *Hymn to Liberty*, the first few stanzas of which were adopted as the national anthem of independent Greece, *On the Death of Lord Byron, Lambros, The Woman of Zante, The Dialogue* and *Porphyros*. A long and unfinished poem called *The Free Besieged* provides a dramatic and symbolic setting for the Siege of Messolonghi by the Turks during the Greek War of Independence.

Andreas Kalvos was also from Zakinthos and he too came under the cultural influences of Italy. His total poetic output in Greek is reflected in twenty odes in an idiosyncratic purist language, written soon after the outbreak of the War of Independence. Kalvos' Greece was the Greece of the western romantic philhellenes and contrasted strongly with the demotic tradition and spiritual vision of Solomos. Almost exclusively his works reflect the ideals and attitudes of phil-hellenism, but his descriptions of the Greek landscape provide a freshness and spontaneity. Another romantic poet was Aristotle Valaoritis (1824–79). A native of Lefkas, he modelled verse on the heroic popular ballads. Lorenzos Mavilis (1860–1912), in contrast, was another champion of demoticism and a disciple of Solomos.

Numerous institutions also took part in the cultural revival on Corfu. New societies included an association for the encouragement of the Greek language and a society whose aim was to translate the Bible into demotic Greek. To these were added the Philological Society, the Ionian Association (founded to promote agriculture, industry and the arts), and a society for the encouragement of music. The latter was established by Nicolas Mantzelos (1795–1873), a composer best-known for the musical score of Solomos' *Hymn of Liberty*. In total the growth in the educated classes, taught in the principles of freedom from the Greek classics and the patriotic stimuli of the poets and writers, were powerful factors in undermining the British protectorate, but Corfu and the islands were to be governed by a further eight High Commissioners before this was finally achieved.

THE REFORMING COMMISSIONERS

Sir Frederick Adam was succeeded by Lord Nugent (1832–5), a nobleman and liberal reformist who had acquired much experience and a reputation as an administrator in the British parliament. He continued Adam's policy of patronising the arts and founded *The Ionian Anthology*, a literary periodical. Through this and various cultural and scientific societies the creative abilities of Corfu and the islands continued to flourish. But Nugent's chief attention was directed to the further improvement of the courts of justice, and acts were passed forbidding the use of Italian when an Ionian was being tried for his life and making it illegal for a judge to preside at a court in his native island. Treasury money, at a low interest rate, was also made available for needy farmers, but the Ionian State was in debt and unable to meet its financial commitments to military and economic works. In 1834 Nugent obtained sanction from the British government for a collective sum of £35,000 annually to meet the deficit in running costs. This was partly used to finance the olive- and currant-growers who were facing a ruinous slump in prices.

Major-General Sir Ward Douglas (1835–41) was a benevolent despot, but the most dynamic and soundest administrator of the islands and the ideal proconsul. During his term of office roads, bridges, prisons, a hospital and a lunatic asylum were built, a cemetery was planned, the water-supply system perfected, and the education system improved. Douglas persevered with the establishment of a national bank and he turned to British funds when efforts to finance it in the islands failed. A prospectus was prepared stressing the trading advantages of the islands with respect to the Mediterranean, the Adriatic and the Levant. It quickly gained strong Ionian and British support and the reliance placed on its issued notes was an important stabilising factor during the British protectorate and afterwards. The Ionian Bank expanded into Greece, Cyprus and Egypt and in 1957 was incorporated into the Ionian and

Popular Bank of Greece. Today, however, the Ionian Bank, London, is completely independent of the Greek branches. One note of discord in Douglas's administration was the serious difference of opinion with the Legislative Assembly over the role of the Senate in the preparation of a new code for civil and criminal law. Following arbitration by the British secretary of state, the Assembly of 1839 was dissolved and a new one called which concurred with the Senate. The revised and edited Ionian law provided greater constitutional freedom and it remains partly in force today. Douglas is commemorated in Corfu by an obelisk on the seafront of Garitsa Bay which records his reforming acts.

The rule of Mackenzie was short (1841–3) but he was liberal and a well-liked ruler and is remembered as being the only High Commissioner after Maitland whose revenue was greater than his expenditure.

Sir John Seaton (1843–9) was perhaps the most extraordinary of them all. He recommended further constitutional changes which included freedom of the Press, an extended suffrage, an electoral system free from government interference and control of the extraordinary expenditure of the state by the Legislative Assembly. Seaton, who had seen in Canada how easily ill-feeling could be averted by a timely concession to the wishes of the people, regarded his reform proposals as a safeguard for the British protectorate. He was bubbling with ideas, but unfortunately the majority proved impractical. The cost of raising one potato on Seaton's model farm was recorded as being one shilling and the prisoners escaped in their dozens from his penitentiary. The penitentiary cost £48,000 and was built in such a position that if Corfu was attacked the gunfire from the fortifications would inevitably destroy it. Seaton also cut a ship canal across the Lefkas lagoon and this again proved disastrous. An English contemporary wrote, 'When the wind is contrary, ships cannot sail into it; when the wind is fair, they will sail around it to avoid the toll.' The free Press which he sanctioned was not slow to criticise him and it is reported that when he learned he was to be replaced 'he hurried the wondering Ionians through more political changes in ten days than England had undergone in ten generations'. Earl Grey (then Colonial Minister), Viscount Kirkwall and others regarded Seaton's reforms as hastily conceived, especially in view of the attack that was now made against the British as oppressors in the free local Press. Seaton's defence appeared in the *Edinburgh Review* of January 1853 where he stressed that in view of the reforms taking place all over Europe it was not possible to maintain a constitution which all knew to be a mockery.

Sir Henry Ward (1849–55) reaped Seaton's whirlwind. Ward's miscalculations and generally bad government led to the cruel suppression of riots which broke out in Cefalonia in August 1849. He is credited with the construction of a road in Corfu, but characteristically this was built with convict labour. Ward was replaced by Sir John Young (1855–8) who turned out to be an uninteresting High Commissioner. According to Jervis 'the cabinets of Europe were surprised at hearing that an English Lord High Commissioner, wearied with the petty vexations of Ionian administration, had advocated the cession of six of the islands to Greece and the conversion of Corfu into a British colony'. The British government disclaimed all connection with his views and he was replaced by William Gladstone (12 November 1858–1 March 1859). Under Gladstone and Sir Henry Storks, the last of the High Commissioners, it became clear that Britain would lose its Ionian protectorate (see Chapter 8).

CRICKET, CAKE AND GINGER-BEER

For almost fifty years (1815–64) the British controlled Corfu and materially, socially and intellectually the island prospered as a British protectorate. Yet it represents a curious episode in the life of the island – often amusing, sometimes bizarre – when the standards and attitudes of Georgian and Victorian Britain were applied to, even forced on, a Mediterranean island community. The Corfiotes, accustomed for centuries to the genial Mediterranean way of life and methods of business, failed to understand the efficiency of the British and to appreciate their standards of justice and honesty. Likewise the British failed to appreciate the national differences in temperament of the islanders and were critical of their lethargy, lack of organisation and love of petty political influence which was often gained through bribery. Writing in 1864 Viscount Kirkwall recalls an earlier incident recorded by Napier which illustrates the attitude of the British Resident to a typically Corfiote situation.

> On one occasion, hearing screams, and learning that a titled Ionian was beating his wife, he rushed into the house, and inflicted on the spot with his riding-whip, a severe personal chastisement on the astonished husband. To be sure, he immediately afterwards sent to offer to the sufferer complete personal satisfaction. But the Ionian, ignorant of Western refinements in such matters, and unused to the pistol, refused to understand how being shot at could fully atone for the disgrace of being flogged.

A further comment by Kirkwall, recommending a friend to rent his own house when visiting the island, illustrates some other problems the British faced. 'In this way', the viscount wrote, 'you escape the oil and garlic flavour which usually permeates all native cookery. . . . The constant use of garlic, and the rare use of soap, impress an Englishman very disagreeably.' Parasites as well as smells were a preoccupation for Anstead although 'fortunately for me', he wrote, 'I am less troubled by unsavoury odours, inasmuch as the peculiar wind of Corfu kept me in a state of perpetual catarrh during the whole time of my visit'!

The British difficulty in adjusting to what appeared to them as extremely foreign conditions led to the emergence of a small and closed society which mixed very little with the natives. This was further divided into civil and military departments and few people were interested in anything beyond their respective professions.

CORFU

Edward Lear, the father of English nonsense rhymes, found Corfu a 'very very very small tittle tattle place' and 'the British habits and way of life on the island monotonous'. Along with the officials, military, naval officers and clergymen came gentlewomen, governesses and nannies from Regency and Victorian England. The ladies set a pattern of social etiquette and decorum and the governesses and nannies demonstrated the principles of strict upbringing of children. Paper-chases on horseback became popular, much to the disgust of the farmers across whose fields these 'wild romps' were organised, and various clubs, a racecourse, and above all, promenading, provided other sporting and leisurely pursuits. It also became customary for British gentlemen to ride out for lunch or dinner to the country-houses of the Graeco–Italian gentry who were often invited to compete in British sporting events. Little of this British culture permeated the rural classes but in the town the islanders learned to drink tea and ginger-beer, to eat beefsteak, plum-cake and apple chutney and to play cricket. At which stage of the protectorate the game became popular cannot be determined, but it has remained as a vital sporting interest to the Corfiotes and many English words related to cricket, but twisted out of recognition, have slipped into the language of the local population. Many of the islanders speak excellent English, a language they prefer to remember than Italian, and it is only comparatively recently that Corfu has adopted the metric system of measurement.

8 A PROVINCE OF GREECE

IN view of its peculiarities, the British occupation of Corfu was discussed in the previous chapter in isolation of the political events that were taking place on the Greek mainland. Beneath Corfu's veneer of economic and social reform a major formative period in the development of modern Greece was underway. The protectorate coincided in time with the struggle for Greek independence from Ottoman domination, and Corfu and the islands were to play significant roles in the revolution. The Ionians enjoyed a higher standard of living and education than their mainland compatriots and the ideas of the French Revolution, enthusiastically received in Greece, were transmitted through both literary and political channels. Byron and other notable campaigning philhellenes spent many weeks in the islands as virtual guests of the Ionian government, although Britain endeavoured to enforce a precarious neutrality to the events of the mainland. In practice this was done in a half-hearted manner, for escape to the Ionian Islands was the most promising way home for Europeans actively engaged in the Greek cause. Corfu also became a refuge for Greeks fleeing from Turkish reprisals. Here they were introduced to European administration, ideals and values, and this was to become the leaven of a regenerated Greece.

JOHN CAPODISTRIAS

A leading figure in the history of modern Greece and Corfu's greatest son is Count John Capo d'Istria. His house is preserved as a monument in Corfu town and his remains are buried in a simple tomb in the seventeenth-century Platytera monastery. Capodistrias, as he later became known, was born in 1776 into an aristocratic family which had moved from Istria to Corfu in the fourteenth century. He was a devout member of the Orthodox Church and was sent to study medicine in Padua before becoming actively involved in the politics of his native islands. Between 1800 and 1807 Capodistrias was a member of the Ionian administrative council and under Mocenigo, a Zantiote in the Russian service, he became the general director of the executive and subsequently secretary of state for foreign affairs, marine and trade. Capodistrias personally directed the defence of Lefkas in 1806 against the threat of Ali Pasha. His suspicion of British intentions in the Ionian Islands was reinforced with Maitland's persuasion of his government to cede Parga to Ali Pasha. Almost the entire population of the town emigrated to Corfu.

Nationalistic aspirations and vigorous defence of the Greek cause brought Capodistrias into close contact with the *klephts*. These were half-brigands, half-Greek patriots who maintained a semi-independent existence in the mountainous regions of the Greek mainland during the Turkish occupation. His friendship with such leaders as Colokotronis and Botsaris was later to prove beneficial although Capodistrias was no warlord. He firmly believed that it was essential for Greece to depend on the protection of a great power and for this reason he joined the service of Russia whose aristocratic and ecclesiastical traditions were similar to his own.

As a diplomat in the service of Tsar Alexander, Capodistrias followed a distinguished career. In 1811 he was appointed attaché to the Russian Embassy in Vienna, a city which was to become a centre for the *Philiki Etairia* (Friendly Society), a secret organisation for the liberation of Greece, founded in Odessa. Capodistrias declined the organisation's leadership and strongly opposed revolutionaries, although his brothers Agostino and Viaro were active members of militant organisations. His subsequent Russian appointments included political correspondent between Vienna and Constantinople and envoy to the Swiss Confederacy. In October 1814 he represented Russia at the Congress of Vienna which made the Ionian Islands an autonomous state under British protection. The British administration failed to match Capodistrias's expectations but events on the Greek mainland were to involve him in the broader issues of the Greek struggle.

The date given for the official uprising of the Greeks against Turkish rule is 25 March 1821. The final victory came as a result of outside aid when a combined British, Russian and French fleet annihilated the Turkish forces at the bay of Navarino in the south-west Peloponnesus (20 October 1827). At an assembly near ancient Troizen, Capodistrias was elected president of the new state although the Greek word *kyvernitis* literally meant governor. His appointment reflected the necessity of securing foreign confidence in the embryonic state, but Capodistrias's main problem was curbing internal feuds and petty factionalism. He argued that Greece could only be governed by a strong central authority and the first two years of his presidency were reasonably successful. His tours of European capitals ensured moral and financial support for Greece but it was chiefly to Corfu and the Ionian Islands that he looked for help. From the islands he brought his brothers and many officials to assist in the running of the state.

In spite of his initial successes, Capodistrias was unable to overcome regional animosity and a violent dispute with the militant clans of Mani in the southern Peloponnesus led to his assassination in Nauplia on 9 October 1831. Ironically Capodistrias was on his way to attend service in the church of St Spiridon, patron saint of his native Corfu. His death was followed by a period of open civil war when British, Russian and French forces again intervened in the affairs of Greece. The Greek crown was offered to Otho, the second son of King Louis of Bavaria, and his small kingdom extended south of a line from the Gulf of Arta in the west to the Gulf of Volos in the east. Otho was seventeen when he arrived in Greece and was entertained in Corfu by Lord Nugent before being escorted to Nauplia by a fleet of Bavarian troops.

ENOSIS

The Greek word for union (or reunion) is *enosis* and it was heard in the Ionian Islands a century before it became a household term in connection with events in twentieth-century Cyprus. The official neutrality of the Ionian state, but the patriotic instincts of the islanders, presented a difficult situation. The British attitude was far from benevolent to Greeks who violated the neutrality ruling, yet it is curious that when Greece achieved independence the Ionian movement for union with the mother-country was slow to gather momentum. Many of the Ionian gentry supported the British policy and others remained loyal in the hope of gaining a title or a KCMG. The landowners and merchants were also dependent on British markets and feared competition from the currant- and olive-oil-producing regions of the mainland. Neither was the authoritarian régime of Otho helpful to the Ionian unionist movement, which to the islanders appeared as foreign as their own British administration. However, a major cause of the apparent apathy, was the British control of the Press. This was so complete that it was impossible for the unionists to propagate their views and ideas.

The movement had gathered momentum by the mid 1840s. Serious disturbances broke out in Cefalonia but Britain, believing that *enosis* was too drastic a solution, advocated constitutional reform instead. Sir John Young, who supported the Ionian claim for union, was replaced by William Gladstone, High Commissioner Extraordinary. His role was that of a pacifier and he arrived in Corfu on 12 November 1858. Gladstone's constitutional measures were so radical that he was besieged by Greeks who regarded him as an 'earthly providence' able to provide administrative places for themselves and even dowries for their daughters! A story, with little foundation, recalls that having failed in his mission he spent the rest of his time on Corfu eating Turkish delight and drinking ginger-beer at the pavement cafés. As a recent writer observes 'to know that a man of such boundless energy was reduced to such a condition may help to lighten the guilt of visitors who usually suffer a similar enervation'.

Sir Henry Storks (1859–64) was the last of the High Commissioners. He carried on bravely maintaining the *status quo* in the face of increasingly vehement demands for union with Greece. Otho's abdication in 1862 provided the way out for Britain. In March 1863 the Greek National Assembly invited Prince William of Denmark to become George I of Greece. In a remarkable expression of goodwill Britain surrendered its protectorate as a coronation present to the new king. The treaty of 29 March 1864 concluded the cession and on 2 June the last Lord High Commissioner left on HMS *Malborough*. *The Times* editorial for 30 July recorded: 'The British flag has been hauled down, not by a victorious enemy, not in ungracious concession to seditious and doleful subjects, but with an air of generosity on the one side, and gratitude on the other, seldom found in international transactions.'

Many Corfiotes looked with sadness on the withdrawal of the British officials and garrison. High-sounding titles were disdained in Athens and the clergy were equally loathe to pass under the control of the Athenian synod and relinquish their large degree of independence granted by the Patriarchate of Constantinople. For Greece too there were problems. The revenue from the Ionian Islands hardly covered their administrative costs, nor did the islands add immediately to the country's military and naval strength. The cession treaty obliged the Greeks to recognise the neutrality of the islands, thus prohibiting their use as naval bases.

Yet for Greece there were obvious advantages stemming from this first acquisition of new territory. The cultural maturity and political experience of the leading Ionian families provided illustrious recruits to the ranks of the administrators and intellectuals. The pattern of Ionian politics had a vastly different tone to any existing in Greece at the period and hence greatly influenced the national political scene. Initially Corfu and the islands retained their own legal and fiscal measures but after 1864, the date of the new Greek constitution, they were gradually eased into the national structure. The Ionian church came under the control of Athens and the Ionian academy was merged with the University of Athens. In 1911 the latter, out of respect for Corfu's earlier cultural lead, changed its name to the National Capodistrian University.

THE ROYAL ISLAND

For a time Corfu continued to flourish economically but the Greek character, summed up by Jervis as 'an indescribable objection to anything practical', gradually took its hold. With the exception of the town's water-supply and the roads, which were maintained after a fashion, the British infrastructure fell into disrepair. 'The Greeks', according to Miller, 'preferred to be governed even less well by their fellow-countrymen . . . than to be better governed by strangers, especially if these were of a different creed.' Corfu, however, continued to maintain the aura of a capital and attracted the wealthy and titled from all parts of Europe. The island's palaces and villas were the summer residences of a number of ruling heads of Europe and prior to World War I Corfu was a select and aristocratic resort. The Palace of St Michael and St George became the official Greek royal residence and the municipality of Corfu offered the villa of Mon Repos to King George I. It passed to his son, Prince Andreas, and was the birthplace of the Duke of Edinburgh.

The strong British attachment to the island also continued and in many ways the nineteenth century laid the foundations for Corfu's present flourishing tourist industry. *The Times* of 4 December 1858 stated:

Corfu has this year been visited by an extraordinary number
of fashionable tourists – political, artistic and sporting . . . the
little town, which covers as much ground as Eaton Square, and
is inhabited by 20,000 persons, has been enlivened by a succession of entertainments and festivities, which have put every
available vehicle into requisition, and must have proved a good
harvest to the vendors of every species of female attire.

But the island had few hotels and a number of visitors bought
or rented country-houses or villas, many dating from the
Venetian period. These still dot the countryside, either isolated
and secluded within their own grounds or attached to villages
which were their former means of support.

Elizabeth of Austria

The Achilleon Palace was the summer retreat of Elizabeth, the
beautiful but restless wife of Franz Josef. Twenty years after
a visit to Corfu in 1861 she commissioned the construction of a
villa 19km from the town, 'a Phaecaean Palace with pillared
collonades and hanging gardens, safe from prying eyes: a
palace worthy of Achilles'. The work was entrusted to the local
consul and to the Italian architect Cardilo. It seems that both
were overawed by the grandeur of the task and produced a
massive Victorian–Baroque confection which hardly matched
the romantic figure of Elizabeth. According to Simpson the
Achilleon is 'the late nineteenth century's idea of the Italian
Renaissance's idea of Greek classicism'.

Dedicated to Achilles, the three-storey palace is decorated
with painted walls and ceilings, heavy marble columns and
golden finery. The floors are reached by a grandiose staircase
at the top of which is a wall-painting of 'The Triumphant
Achilles' by the Austrian Franz Mats. Throughout the palace
the current motifs are dolphins which were sacred to Thetis,
Achilles' mother. Undistinguished statues adorn the ornamental gardens and represent the mythology and ancient
history of Greece. 'The Dying Achilles', the work of Ernest

Herter, expresses more than anything the temperament and romantic character of Elizabeth.

Elizabeth's unhappy and lonely life was ended by her assassination in Geneva in 1898. The Achilleon was inherited by her daughter, a princess of Bavaria, but it remained little used for a number of years. At the suggestion of King George of Greece it was purchased by Kaiser Wilhelm II.

The Kaiser
Wilhelm's memoirs describe his fascination for the scenery of Corfu and his interest in the Achilleon 'in which the Empress and himself could rest every spring, after the hard winters of Berlin'. The palace took on a Germanic air with heavy furnishings and structural alterations which partly transformed it into a royal office. From 1908 to 1914 the Kaiser arrived in April with his entire court, bringing presents for the 'natives'. On one occasion the gifts of soap did little to increase his popularity! But what offended the tastes of the Corfiotes most was his replacement of 'The Dying Achilles' by a colossal prefabricated warlike Achilles, the work of the German sculptor Godz. On it was placed the inscription: 'From the greatest German to the greatest Greek.'

During World War I the Achilleon was used as a military hospital and was then confiscated by the Greek state. Much of its furniture and lavish equipment was auctioned. In 1961 the Greek government accepted a proposal to turn the Achilleon into a casino and to many the supreme essay in bad taste has at long last found its true *métier*. 'To walk round this morgue of faded majesty', states Guy Pentreath (*Hellenic Traveller*), 'is to see a classic example of bathos. But Fortune's revolving wheel has recently turned it into a casino.' Parts of the ground floor are kept as a museum and display some of the personal effects of Elizabeth and the Kaiser. These include a fine portrait of Wilhelm by Winterhalter and the saddle throne from which he dictated his despatches. Perhaps the most poignant item is a gold coin originally belonging to Elizabeth's brother-in-law Maximilian,

Archduke of Austria and Emperor of Mexico. It was one of the coins given by Maximilian to the soldiers who, under Juarez, formed his firing-squad at Querataro on 19 June 1867. It appears that the vain Maximilian had bribed the soldiers to fire at his heart and not his face. One of the coins was returned to Elizabeth.

CORFU DURING THE WARS

In 1914, fifty years after the union with Greece, the status of the Ionian Islands was challenged in a boundary dispute between Greece and Albania. Diplomatic manoeuvres were postponed by the outbreak of World War I and in 1916 Corfu became a base for the reorganisation of the Serbian army. Assailed from the north by Austria, the Serbs retreated across Albania and were evacuated to French-held Corfu. Some 155,000 Serbs were quarantined on the island but many failed to recover from the effects of months of forced marching in the bitter cold of the Balkan winter. Overcrowding and disease led to heavy mortality estimated at one-third of the army and the Serbian cemetery is located on the island of Vido. By July, however, the remainder had recovered sufficiently for active service.

On 20 July 1917 Corfu again played an active role in Balkan politics. The Pact of Corfu was an agreement signed between Prime Minister Pasic of Serbia and Ante Trumbic, President of the Yugoslav Committee. The Committee was established in London in 1815 and was an organisation working for the reunification of South Slav peoples into one state. The Pact proclaimed that Serbs, Croats, Slovenes and Montenegrins should form one state under the Serbian dynasty, but each having a democratic constitution and local autonomy. Thus the Pact of Corfu formed the basic charter of unity for Yugoslavia which became a reality when the Serbian army marched triumphantly back to Belgrade in November 1918.

The Corfu Incident

After World War I, Greek territorial claims were shaped by

the allies, especially Britain. Moves into northern Epirus, however, were blocked by Italy which acted as an agent for the new Albanian régime. A Graeco–Albanian frontier commission was established by the League of Nations but its work was disrupted by the now-famous 'Corfu Incident' of 1923. This involved the assassination on Greek soil of the Italian delegate and the members of his staff. Mussolini held the Greek government responsible and retaliated by bombarding and occupying Corfu town, together with Paxos, Antipaxos and the small islands to the north. Pressure from the League of Nations persuaded Mussolini to evacuate the islands on 27 September, but not before Greece acceded to a number of Italian demands, including the payment of a considerable indemnity. Corfu remained a 'frontier region' until the 1960s and a state of war still technically exists between Greece and Albania.

The Italians returned to Corfu in 1941–3. This followed their invasion of Greece from Albania. Mussolini had expected little resistance but all Italian counter-offensives were beaten back in what was virtually a spontaneous uprising by the Greeks. Germany saved Mussolini from total humiliation and the Adriatic coastline was divided into segments over which Italy obtained either 'sovereignty' or 'influence'. Similar to their policies in the Dodecanese, Italian public notices appeared on Corfu claiming that the island had always been Italian. An Italian governor was appointed and Italian currency and postage stamps were introduced. Corfu was again fortified but in September 1943, following the Anglo–Italian Armistice, the island failed to defend itself against German landings. The town suffered ten days of bombardment before falling to the Germans and the damage was extensive. In 1944 the Germans evacuated the island with the arrival of the British.

International incidents involving Corfu since World War II are few and trivial. In 1947 there was a scene in the Corfu Channel when mines laid by the Albanians caused damage and casualties aboard a British man-of-war, but most of the island's modern development has been linked with the political events

Plate 25 (right) A wayside shrine at the entrance to the village of Kinopiastes

Plate 26 (below) The small fishing settlement at Ipsos

Plate 27 A back-street transaction in the old town of Corfu

Plate 28 Numerous festivals provide frequent opportunities for the display of local costumes. (*M. Pechliranidis*)

of mainland Greece. Perhaps the most amusing 'takeover' attempt occurred in 1969 when the self-styled 'Commodore' Hubbard made a bid to convert the old royal Palace into a University of Scientology. Although supported by a number of traders and merchants his proposition was unacceptable.

9   THE CHURCH, SAINTS AND THE FAMILY

IN spite of a long history of foreign control, the native culture of the Corfiotes has remained remarkably unscathed. All the occupying powers have left physical and cultural reminders of their influence on the island yet the contemporary population is essentially Greek in character, and customs and traditions handed down over the centuries continue to form the bases of everyday life. This corporate existence and consciousness of ethnic and spiritual unity with other Greeks was sustained by the use and practice of the Greek language and the Orthodox faith. Both have been powerful factors in ensuring the cultural survival, especially among the rural classes, and they can be regarded as the essential pillars or coefficients of Hellenism.

The moral keynote of the Ionian agitation for union with Greece was not so much liberty as nationality based on language and religion. Reference has already been made to the role played by Corfu and the islands in the development of the modern Greek novel and poetry. This was achieved by the revival of the common demotic tongue as a language of literary expression. These channels of Greek patriotism were reinforced by the vitality of the church. In allowing the Greek Church to maintain its traditions and the peasantry their local customs, Venice had assured the preservation of both language and faith and the unique identity of the islanders as Greeks. The position of the church was strengthened during the brief period of the Heptanesus Republic and it was the French attitude towards Greek religion which antagonised the rural classes against them. History has proved that foreign government in Greece

THE CHURCH, SAINTS AND THE FAMILY

succeeds only if its policies are tolerant to the national church and clergy. It is significant, therefore, that the French occupations of the Ionian Islands were of short duration.

THE ORTHODOX CHURCH

Corfu is predominantly an Orthodox society although there are Roman Catholic, Protestant and Jewish minorities, the latter forming a community of about 150. Many Jews were forced to leave during World War II and their present social and economic role in no way compares to their importance under the Angevins and Venetians. The majority of the Roman Catholics are not descendants of early Venetian families, as one would expect, but of the Maltese farmers and builders who were brought to the island in the nineteenth century along with Italian artisans. One of Greece's three Roman Catholic archbishops resides in Corfu and the cathedral holds daily services and liturgies. The Anglican Church of the Holy Trinity normally functions from Easter to the end of September, coinciding with the main influx of British visitors. Corfu also has its Evangelical Church which holds regular services.

Orthodoxy has remained a vital force in the lives of the Corfiote people since the martyrdoms of St Sosipatros and St Jason. Curiously, regular churchgoing affects only a small percentage of the population although few would regard themselves as non-believers. Orthodox Churches hold regular daily services and a common sight is the procession of worshippers, chiefly women, offering prayers and dedications to the icons and other revered relics. The daily, weekly and annual cycles of the liturgy form the bases of the corporate and social act of common worship and the building in which they are celebrated must be of central importance. Whether in the town or the countryside the Corfiotes are proud of their churches and even the humblest village lavishes gifts for the adornment of its church.

Greece is now the only country in the world that is officially an Orthodox Christian country. The liturgy of the church is the whole complex of rite and worship inherited directly from Byzantium and still involves the same forms and rubrics as those used in early times. This amazing continuity can be traced back to at least the sixth century AD and the foundation of Orthodoxy itself to the teachings of St Paul. This is not to suggest that some customs have not changed or been modified, for a number of pagan rites have been translated into occasions of religious significance. Worship in rural areas is often a sort of 'primitive' Orthodoxy allied to folklore, superstition and the 'evil eye'. Each village and each seasonal activity – harvesting, sowing, fishing and travelling – have their own patron saints whose attributes and miraculous powers have their counterparts in the gods and demi-gods of antiquity.

Orthodox bishops and other high officials are celibate and are recruited from monastic institutions. Monasticism, therefore, plays a major role in Orthodoxy and in the past was a vital force in preserving the religious heritage during foreign rule. Corfu has a large number of monasteries, many with interesting architecture, histories, frescoes and legends. The local populations are in close touch with the monasteries to which pilgrimages are frequently made.

The local priest or *papas* is allowed to marry and normally he lives a similar existence to the ordinary villager. He usually supplements his income from the land or by running a small business. His level of education is generally above that of his parishioners, hence he has their confidence and his council is respected and valued. Marriage prevents the *papas* from rising higher in the church hierarchy and he is not allowed to preach. Instead he reads a circular sermon sent to him by the bishop. As nation and church are hard to distinguish in Greece, this circular can be as much a political treatise as an exhortation to worship and serve God!

THE CHURCH, SAINTS AND THE FAMILY

CHURCH ARCHITECTURE AND DESIGN

The traditional form of the Orthodox Church, current throughout Greece until the seventeenth century, is the cross-in-square structure surmounted by a central dome. Its impression of architectural simplicity is deceptive and symbolically the dome and cross mark the union of heaven and earth, or the two natures of the incarnate Christ. Largely because of the Catholic domination of Corfu from the Angevin period of the nineteenth century, the only surviving example of this true Byzantine-styled church is that of St Jason and St Sosipatros at Anemomilos which dates from the twelfth century. Its interior walls, once covered with frescoes, are now bare, and its icons belong to later centuries. However, the masonry of the external walls, with their intricate designs of red tiles, illustrate something of the ornate detail that accompanied the medieval Byzantine church.

Byzantine architecture was replaced on Corfu by what has been termed the 'Ionian–Baroque' church of the seventeenth and eighteenth centuries. Young describes its structure as a 'tall shoe-box, lit by segmented side windows, and covered with a pitched roof of tiles ending in triangular gables'. The roof form was later modified and the structure itself had its precedent in the ruined sixth-century basilica of Palaeopolis. Ionian–Baroque architecture is also distinguished by its belfry which is usually a free-standing campanile topped with a painted dome. It is exemplified in St Spiridon's Church in Corfu town and in the Platytera monastery on its outskirts. Byzantine-styled belfrys generally consisted of an ornamental wall pierced with arches for bells. They stood either above the façade of the church or over its courtyard gate. As a traditional design this has persisted to the present day, especially in the countryside.

The Church of St Spiridon, which houses the remains of the island's patron saint, follows Young's description of Ionian–

Baroque architecture except that a flat ceiling covers the single-aisled basilica. Building began in 1596 on the site of an earlier foundation and although the exterior appears dull and uninteresting it is compensated by the sumptuousness, if a little overdone, of its interior. The chief features of the Church of St Spiridon include an impressive stone screen and a gilt-scrolled and painted panelled ceiling (1699–1729) which was re-decorated in the nineteenth century. The Platytera monastery, founded in 1716, also has a fine screen and carvings and con-tains many paintings from the Ionian school which incor-porated the artistic tenets of Crete. Other town churches, including the Orthodox and Catholic Cathedrals, the Pando-crator and Panagia Kremasti (both in the Campiello district), together with many monasteries and churches in the country-side, are rich in architectural and artistic embellishments.

The interior design of most Corfiote churches follows a traditional and symbolic pattern. The main body of the church, the nave, is separated from the altar or sanctuary by a tall screen (the *iconostasis*) beyond which only the priest is normally allowed to enter. Symbolically the separation of priest from congregation represents the division between the divine and the human, or the spiritual and sensible worlds. Yet at the same time it unites the two for the screen is adorned with icons which portray this double function, representing the world of imagination that stands midway between the sensible and spiritual. Icons are also placed on stands and on walls, and often the whole interior wall-surface of the church is decorated with frescoes. Therefore, the veneration of holy images is a central aspect of the Orthodox ritual. They are regarded as testimonies of the process of transfiguration and in them is felt to be present something of the deified reality of the prototypes – Christ, the Virgin, angels and saints. Many are covered with small silver votives, the intention being to put a prayer into visual form. These may be small images of a sailor or a soldier for whose safety the parents or family is concerned. A limb, a hand, a heart or a body represent prayers for the recovery of health. Eventually these simulacra are melted down to add more silver adornment to their respective icons.

Thus in its architecture and decoration the Greek Orthodox Church is a visible projection of the spiritual world. The Greeks are fervent believers in divine-human co-operation and in the former's intervention. All faculties, physical and mental, are used in worship – hence the need for icons, incense, candles, colours and chanting.

FEASTS AND FESTIVALS

Corfu is characterised by a large number of feast days or *panagiri* which usually combine a religious festival at a local church or monastery with an excuse for eating, drinking, folk-singing and dancing in traditional dress. The rich peasant costumes, rarely seen except on special occasions, are among the most colourful in Greece and there is considerable local variation in the style and trimmings of the women's dress. Corfiote costumes are remarkable for their rich display of jewellery and headdresses. The latter take the form of turbans encircling the head and composed of brilliantly coloured ribbons entwined with hair. They bear a striking resemblance to the Venetian courtesan's dress of bygone days. Women's bodices, skirts and aprons are equally colourful, the former richly embroidered in gold and silver thread motifs. Skirts are highly pleated and braided and even the more simple aprons carry rich decoration. The men's costume, traditionally less colourful, is equally distinctive. It is composed of baggy knee-length breeches, long socks, evzone-style shoes, bolero jackets, loose-fitting shirt and wide-brimmed hat. Less pretentious but equally traditional apparel can be seen in many villages as part of everyday dress. This is worn only by the older women of the interior villages and consists of a black skirt and over-skirt, a loose white cotton blouse with a drawstring neck and full sleeves, a black bodice and a white headkerchief.

It is difficult to say exactly how many feast days are celebrated on Corfu for there are some 800 churches and each day is liable to be some saint's day when a *panagiri* takes place. This fact illustrates how religion and the saintly hegemony obtrude into everyday life. Churches dedicated to St Mary, St Nicholas, St George, St John and of course St Spiridon, are responsible for major celebrations throughout the island, whilst the lesser-known saints days often pass unnoticed, except locally. All over the island, on mountain tops or on lonely headlands overlooking the sea, there are shrines and small chapels dedicated to saints. These too have their day, even if they fail to attract large crowds. All *panagiri* are occasions for religious worship, but a visit to the local church which is especially decorated for the occasion is accompanied by dancing to a string band, hawkers peddling trinkets, an abundance of local wine and spirits and the inevitable lamb roasting on a spit. The festivities usually last all night and perhaps the most incongruous sight is the traditionally dressed middle-aged villagers mingling with the jean-clad youth.

Easter is the main feast of the Orthodox year and on Corfu it is celebrated with the same pomp, dignity and fervour common throughout Greece. There are some intriguing customs, however, for in Corfu town many doorways carry crosses marked in blood. This appears to be a Christian adaptation of the Jewish passover ritual. Another curious custom occurs at precisely 11 am on Easter Sunday when old pots and plates are thrown from the upper storeys of houses to smash on the pavements below. The precise reason for this spectacle is vague but it is probably a token version of the gauntlet the Jews had to run in the Middle Ages if they ventured into the streets during Holy Week.

The Greek Orthodox Easter is calculated in a complicated manner and its date, still based on the Julian-style calandar, can occur up to a month later than in Western Christendom. By edict of the pope Catholics in Corfu conform to the Orthodox Easter, but the Protestant minority celebrate it on the normal prescribed day for the West. An almost extinct group known as the 'old calendarites' refuse to conform to the Western calendar and still keep to the old style. During Wheeler's time this caused serious problems and until 1923 the Orthodox calendar was always a fortnight later than the Western calendar – a point to remember when Wheeler mentions dates. 'For example in Corfu', states Forte (*Wheeler on Corfu*), 'the time/date of 12.30 am Monday, 28 December in the year 1899 was in effect 11.30 pm on Sunday, 10 January in the year 1900 in London.'

On Corfu Easter involves as much preparation in the kitchen as Christmas does in Western Europe and work starts at least ten days before the events. On Maundy Thursday the Paschal lamb is killed and hung until Saturday when Easter soup is prepared from its organs and entrails. Friday is a day of universal mourning and most churches have their evening *Epitaphios* procession when the flower-covered symbolical bier of Christ is followed by the clergy, church dignitaries and the general population. Forte's description of the subsequent Saturday events are the most graphic and atmospheric:

> at midnight when the bishop, standing on a raised dais in the centre of the multitude, reads his solemn benediction, all the lights in the town and on ships at sea become illuminated. . . . The great Venetian fort, until now a dark and forbidding mass on the skyline, shines forth with the words 'Christos Anesti' – 'Christ has Risen'. The tiny bobbing weaving candles, which are in fact people, now hurry home, taking good care that the precious flame will not die before they reach their destination.

Less emphasis is now placed on fasting and this is the time for a celebration meal with the whole of Sunday spent in eating, drinking and dancing. In the villages lamb, basted with lemon juice and olive oil, is slowly cooked over an open spit and then eaten with copious quantities of wine and spirits. Numerous visitors, especially Athenians, visit Corfu for the Easter celebrations which are reputed to be the most moving and entertaining in Greece.

Easter is just one of the island's many religious festivals. Of equal importance are the annual events which mark the procession of St Spiridon through the streets of Corfu. Like Easter they attract large crowds, both local and from other parts of Greece.

ST SPIRIDON

'The island is really the Saint,' states Lawrence Durrell, 'and the Saint is the island.' The saint in question is Spiridon who like all Greek saints is the worker of miracles, although he has strong Ionian rivals in Cefalonia's St Yerasimos and in Zakinthos's St Dionysius. By his miraculous intervention he is believed to have saved the town once from famine and twice from major epidemics of the plague. When the great plague of Naples struck Corfu it was Spiridon who dismissed it in the shape of an eagle. The saint was awarded his own church in 1596 and his gratitude and protective powers were again revealed in 1716 when he engineered the defeat of the besieging Turks, as mentioned earlier. His most recent intervention was in 1944 when the Germans and Italians fought for the possession of the town and the island. Corfu was partly destroyed in the shelling, but the Church of St Spiridon and those who took refuge in it remained unharmed. For the contemporary sceptic there is a booklet sold at the church which records more minor miracles – a policeman cured of epilepsy; the evil-eye averted; an old man cured of the 'distressing' gift of tongues, and there is further evidence of his dealings against croup, diphtheria and lice!

Not surprisingly the cult of Corfu's patron saint is strong and powerful. The island and the saint are synonymous and his influence permeates every aspect of life, embodying the Corfiote's loves, hopes and fears in an adoration that is often independent of religious sentiment. Numerous male children are named after him and Spiridoula is a common name among girls. This ubiquitous name, as Young records, can lead to utter confusion. 'If one were to call "Spiro!" loudly in a restaurant, the owner, two of the waiters, five people at nearby tables, the itinerant seller of lottery tickets and the dozing cab-driver outside would probably all look round.' Coastal craft carry his religious mementos, for he is also patron of the Corfu seas, he protects bus-drivers on the island's precarious roads (and hopefully their passengers) and his name in an oath symbolises the most solemn of vows. It has been said that in St Spiridon the Corfiotes have a non-appointed director of all their affairs and four times a year in token of their respect his mummified body is carried around the town in a glass-fronted palaquin. The saint is preceded by bands and followed by officials, dignitaries, contingents of the armed services, boy scouts and girl guides, and schoolchildren in their Sunday best. The saint is borne under an old canopy of crimson and gold, supported by silver poles and accompanied by priests – incongruously, for a mummified body, it is a type of sedan chair.

The Spiridon processions on Palm Sunday, Easter Even, 11 August and the first Sunday in November are major Corfiote occasions and reveal a mixture of Orthodox ritual, Venetian civic pomp and Victorian brass-bands. These full honours were accorded the saint by most of Corfu's occupying and protecting powers but the British involvement in the processions earned acid comments in Murray's *Handbook* of 1840:

> The absurd affectation of compliance with the prejudices of the people, which occasions much annoyance to both officers and men, has been adopted with a view to conciliate the affections of the natives. One is indeed led to doubt the motives of the British when, according to the description of Private Wheeler in 1823, the Saint, before the start of the procession, was placed upright by the grand altar at which moment the guard presented arms, and the band played 'God save the King', and a nearby battery let off a Royal salute.

The life of Spiridon and his miraculous adventures are regarded by many as an amusing study in myth, although fragmentary references in early documents provide a bare guide to his origins and career. He was not a Corfiote but according to Butler's *Lives of the Saints* a Cypriot, and tradition names the small village of Trimithion, near Nicosia, as his birthplace. Initially he lived the life of a shepherd and on the death of his wife entered a monastery. Subsequently he became bishop of an obscure rural diocese but played a leading role in the Ecumenical Council of Nicaea in AD 325. A long life, many good works and numerous miracles (including one resurrection!) contributed to his popularity, so that on death he became venerated as a saint. For some time his remains rested in the church at Trimithion, but were later transferred to Constantinople with the fall of Cyprus to the Saracens. When the Turks threatened Constantinople his remains, and those of St Theodora Augusta, were acquired by Kalocheiritis who is said to have been both a Greek priest and a wealthy citizen. The two saints were brought to Corfu in sacks slung on the sides of mules. The remains of St Theodora were given to the community and now rest in the Orthodox Cathedral, but Spiridon was a source of revenue and awe. The eldest sons of Kalocheiritis were given half shares in the embalmed body and when these shares were 'united' in the possession of Philip, the grandson, an unsuccessful attempt was made to carry off the body to Venice. Spiridon then became a dowry for Philip's daughter Asimeri and was married, so to speak, into the Voulgaris family. A church was built for Spiridon in the sixteenth century but not until as recently as 1925 did he pass to the control of the Orthodox Church.

Finally nationalised, St Spiridon is a small dried-up mummy lying at rest for most of the year in a silver coffer. His withered feet are clad in embroidered slippers and protrude from a vent at the bottom of the sarcophagus. The nearby screen is hung with a profusion of lamps and silver votive offerings which the faithful have placed to prompt his answering of prayers. The Greeks stoop and kiss his slippers after he has returned from the processions in a manner that has changed little from Wheeler's day – 'Greeks in their pious zeals struggling and swearing with each other to get to the Saint first.'

THE CHURCH, SAINTS AND THE FAMILY

Whereas at least in village society the church is the communal centre of gravity, the focal point in ordinary Corfiote life is the family circle. This is often large and extends far beyond the precepts of Western society. The family unit consists not merely of the husband, wife and children, but extends through a whole range of relatives to second cousins and even further. Three even four generations living under the same roof are common, for old people are automatically taken care of within the family and the opinions of grandparents are respected and valued. In the same vein, children, especially during their earlier years, are enormously indulged by their parents and are the objects of almost unconditional affection and admiration. Many would say that this adoration often approaches idolatory, especially in the case of a son.

The family functions as an immensely strong and rigid social unit and although old ways are gradually dying out, parochial ties and attitudes are very marked and family loyalties take precedence over all others. However the family is not simply a domestic association based on blood relationship but a corporate enterprise uniting to provide for the subsistence of its members. This may involve exploitation of its fields and flocks, or work in the town, and often both. It is also a religious community protected by its personal icons and other sacred objects. The house itself is a sanctuary for its members and guests. It is this multiform character that underlies the exclusive solidarity of the family, even within a tightly knit village community. As such each member is obliged to give help to another, including financial assistance in times of need.

One of the main concerns of the Corfiote family is the marriage and honourable establishment of the children. This is often a crucial test of the family's resources and reputation. For girls the provision of a dowry is still a prerequisite and although the custom of collecting donations at the infant girl's

139

christening has largely lapsed, a substantial dowry is traditional and marriage prospects are often dependent on the wealth of the parents. In the town, but to a lesser extent in the countryside, the daughter has some say in the choice of a marriage partner; but it is the father who has the responsibility for conducting the matrimonial proceedings. These are governed by complex points of procedure and ritual and often require the services of an intermediary so that any breakdown in negotiations will not bring humiliation to either side. The dowry itself consists of household goods but often land, livestock and a house are prerequisites. Money is becoming a more common demand in the countryside as it has long been in the town.

In the villages the marriage feast which follows the traditional Orthodox wedding service is held in the local taverna and is accompanied by song and dance. Such proceedings are lengthy but local customs have changed so considerably that as Forte confirms, 'it is not an uncommon sight to see an eight month pregnant bride dressed in virgin white leading the dance after the wedding feast'. In fairness, however, chastity or at least prudent behaviour is highly prized among Corfiote girls and is the major, sometimes the only, part of their dowry. Family life rests on the Greek tenet of *philotimo* or honour which governs the whole status of inter-family relationships and also the status of the family within the village, district and region. Dishonour to oneself brings dishonour to the family and hence the loss of self-esteem to all concerned.

10   OLIVES AND TOURISTS

THE basic characteristics of the Corfiote economy are those traditionally associated with other Greek island communities. The major differences are related to Corfu's greater fertility and productivity, both within the Ionian archipelago and especially in comparison with Aegean Greece, and its increasing reliance on the tourist trade. In the case of the latter, Corfu may be compared to Greek islands such as Rhodes, Myconos and Crete where the tourist industry is a major source of income, beneficial to the local balance of payments and a major factor in general economic development. After World War II the economy increasingly orientated itself towards the improvement of its agricultural production, to the establishment of agriculturally based industries and to the improvement of its tourist infrastructure. Agricultural yield has almost doubled and new hotels and roads to natural beauty-spots have opened up formerly inaccessible areas as vacation centres. Foreign currency from tourism annually exceeds £3 million and equals about half the revenue from agriculture. Tourism itself has greatly increased the demand for a number of agricultural products, especially fruit, vegetables and dairy produce.

Of Corfu's active population 70 per cent is engaged in agriculture, which officially defined by Greek standards includes the subsidiary occupations of forestry and fishing. The remainder is divided between services (19 per cent) and industry and manufacturing (11 per cent). Agriculture therefore is the mainstay of the island and Corfu's rural population density is the highest in Greece. It averages 119·5 persons per sq km compared to 64 persons for Greece as a whole. In spite of the island's comparative richness this density is considerable in relation to the available resources and marked economic and social disparities exist between Corfu town and the countryside. Agricultural incomes are small and inadequate to meet the growing demands of farmers to improve their economic situation or to provide a better education and social status for their children. The rural–urban gulf is intensified by the fact that the tourist industry is concentrated in and around Corfu town, or at selective scenic spots and coastal locations. Although tourist demand naturally has its effect on rural production the inequalities between capital and countryside are widening. The result is a declining rural population as increasing numbers find seasonal or permanent jobs in Corfu town, or move to Athens or abroad. Electric power is now supplied to most rural communities and major improvements have been made to water-supplies, but despite these innovations rural life, especially in winter, is rigorous. The picture of the Corfiote village preserving a rural simplicity and housing a friendly and hospitable population should not cloud the fact that many pressing social and economic problems remain unsolved.

THE RURAL SCENE

Much of the character and beauty of the Corfiote landscape are due to the general absence of extensive cultivation and the apparent abandonment of the land to its natural state. Large areas of the island are in fact overgrown with semi-natural vegetation, but this deceptively shields from view the small pockets of cultivated and intensively farmed land which at the same time merges with olive groves and other fruit orchards. It was this characteristic which caught the attention of the nineteenth-century visitor D. T. Anstead. 'It is not the fashion in this island', he stated, 'to construct hedges or walls, or ditches, or any other limits of property, the whole place becoming one unbroken olive forest for miles and miles together.'

According to Anstead the general state of the island 'was the product of the Corfiote's idleness, leaving the land to the accidents of time and weather'. His statements must be qualified, if not disputed, for the island's 'wild civility' is the result of a complex set of factors, not least the confused and detailed character of its topography which produces a succession of small natural units devoted to a variety of crops. The fact remains, however, that during certain seasons it is often difficult to distinguish farmed from uncultivated land and the most lasting impression is that of an overgrown parkland.

Since antiquity Corfu's rural economy has been basically a dry-farming agriculture dominated by the classic Mediterranean crops, olives, vines and grains. General agricultural mismanagement has not left the island unscathed and soil exhaustion, deforestation and erosion have greatly reduced the area which may be cultivated. Considerable efforts have been expended on land improvement and in particular on drainage, irrigation and flood protection. Hillside terracing, one traditional method, has brought new land into cultivation. Terraces on steep slopes are constructed from the ample material provided by the rocky subsoil and are filled with soil from the lower slopes and valley bottoms. The root systems of fruit trees, particularly the olive, help to consolidate the terrace for the cultivation of grains and other crops. These grow beneath the trees in a system of inter-cropping found throughout the island. The scarcity of water, resulting from seasonal rainfall and steep run-off, is also diminished by terracing and, where possible, water shortages are compensated locally by well water and irrigation. But on Corfu only 12,200 acres, or 14 per cent of the cultivated area, is irrigated and much of this is confined to the Ropa and Mesolongi lowlands and to the neighbourhood of Corfu town, especially the area fringing the Chalikiopoulos lagoon. The silting up of this lagoon has been accelerated by the construction of a 700 metre-long dyke leaving only restricted communications with the sea. From the lagoon irrigation channels feed the market-gardening areas and the supply of water is rationally managed by the small proprietors. With few other exceptions irrigation is purely local and small scale, although co-operation and communal action could significantly increase the irrigated acreage.

The principal area of land reclamation is the Ropa valley which during the early years of this century formed an extensive marsh with temporary lakes around its borders. The initial drainage work was undertaken in 1904 and consisted of a main water channel, 7km long, to Ermones Bay. The permanent swamp was drained but the capacity of the canal was insufficient to prevent winter flooding and consequently the land was used for pasture rather than cultivation. Further work in the thirties led to more successful drainage and the Ropa valley has developed into a major cereal and vine-producing region. Today it is a mosaic of fields surrounded by olive groves and shared by a number of hillside settlements including the villages of Giannades and Liapades. The Ropa valley is Corfu's best-known reclamation project but other drainage schemes, albeit smaller, are numerous. Another feature of the island are the small dams built across torrent courses to retain water during the rainy season.

A major change in the rural scene has been the break-up of the large estates which dated from the Venetian period. On these the peasant farmers had been serfs and the aristocracy spent little on updating methods or improving amenities. The decline of the large estates followed the establishment of the modern state and was accelerated by two factors. Prior to union, land inheritance was handed down on the male side only, but after 1864 it was divided equally between male and female descendants in accordance with Greek inheritance and dowry laws. Secondly the landed aristocracy was not recognised as a distinct class in the modern Greek state and the Corfiote nobility declined. Territorial family alliances became fewer and hastened the break-up of the landed estates. Influential Corfiote names still survive but not everyone bearing such a distinction is necessarily a descendant from a ruling family. Over the years peasants often acquired the name of the owner on whose land they worked.

The replacement of estates by small peasant farms brought mixed blessings for Greek inheritance and dowry laws have produced extremely small agricultural holdings consisting of a variety of dispersed plots. For sons and daughters who remain in the countryside the family asset, which must be generally divided, is land. Since land comes into the family with daughters-in-law (as part of the dowry) and leaves it with daughters, the combination of customs has produced farm holdings of extreme fragmentation. The effect has been heightened through time by the absolute shortage of cultivable land. Although there is legislation for voluntary land consolidation the technical and social consequences of the holding system are very marked. Much of the working day is spent in travelling with implements to and from dispersed plots, many of which can lie in different directions from the villager's home. Thus round-trips of 20km are not uncommon.

Where land is fragmented the use of modern machinery is difficult for the small and irregularly shaped fields, bounded by those of neighbours, are usually without track access. Irrigation, crop spraying, weeding and measures to prevent soil erosion therefore depend on the goodwill of the adjacent farmer. Another disadvantage is that animals cannot be systematically grazed on small, dispersed and unfenced plots whose boundaries are often a source of dispute and litigation. Apart from land fragmentation, Corfiote agriculture has other deficiencies. Inappropriate farming methods and the practice of continually planting cereal crops instead of proper rotations has exhausted the soil. The use of chemical fertilisers is insufficient and the ratio of farm expenditure to gross value of production is low.

MAJOR CROPS

Statistics (1974) issued by the Greek Ministry of Agriculture reveal that 78,977 acres or 59 per cent of the island's total area is cultivated, a figure which includes large areas devoted to olive groves and other fruit orchards. A breakdown of the percentage areas devoted to the major crops is as follows:

	Area in acres	Per cent of cultivated area
Olives	37,500	48·0
Vines	14,025	17·6
Cereals	9,720	12·1
Fruits	5,032	6·2
Green vegetables	5,050	6·1
Potatoes	4,215	5·1
Fodder crops	1,675	2·3
Tobacco	217	0·5
Other crops	1,543	2·1
Total	78,977	100·0

The official statistics also indicate that a further 50,760 acres or 32 per cent of the island's total area is capable of being cultivated and the remainder is classified as 'woodland' or unproductive land. The latter categories, however, also comprise much of the island's pasturage for the Greek definition of pasture is a wide one and generally refers to residual categories of land.

On Corfu an increasing specialisation in market-orientated products has tended to break down the traditional Mediterranean crop complex, although olives, vines and, to a lesser extent, grains remain the bases of the average islander's diet and cash income. Corfiote agriculture is based chiefly on tree crops and may be further subdivided into extensive and intensive methods of exploitation. The former mainly concerns olive production and the latter principally viticulture and citrusfruit cultivation, but other generalisations become irrelevant for the traditional peasant response to his environment is polyculture or mixed cultivation devoted to a variety of crops. The philosophy of growing a 'bit of everything' is one that appeals to the farmer, although Corfiote polyculture cannot be accounted for solely in human terms. It is as much a product of the variety of physical conditions encountered within the island, particularly those that relate to soil differences, micro-climates and the conditions of slope, altitude and aspect.

THE OLIVE

'Dominant in a landscape of richer greens, the olive', writes Lawrence Durrell, 'is for the peasant both a good servant and a hard master.' On Corfu it plays a principal role in agriculture and since antiquity has been the traditional mainstay of the rural economy. Olive groves are present on all but the steepest and most inaccessible slopes and it is estimated that the island has over 3·5 million cultivated trees and an indeterminate number growing wild among the *maquis* and in natural groves. The olive's green-grey foliage and its gnarled hollowed trunk often reaches great heights and from a distance the groves appear as impenetrable forests. In fact most of the trees have been carefully planted in serried ranks to form extensive orchards. This pattern dates back to antiquity although the predominance of the tree is a legacy of the Middle Ages when its cultivation was encouraged by the Venetians. Land values were, and often still are, computed on the basis of the size of the olive grove.

Although a drought-resisting tree adapted to the Mediter-ranean climate, the olive needs to be well spaced out for full production and to ensure an adequate supply of ground water. The classical agronomists were well aware of this requirement and Solon recommended a minimum distance of 9ft between each tree. Columella prescribed intervals that ranged from 25 to 40ft especially when crops were grown between the rows. The method of inter-cropping between olives is a usual practice for the tree's thin foliage does not stint the ground-crops of sunlight. At best the olive is slow growing and takes between seven and twelve years after planting to produce a crop, and up to thirty years to attain full maturity and productivity. The gathering season begins in November and can continue until

May. This is advantageous to the farmer for the olive's peak labour demand comes when all other harvests are completed.

The Peasant's Security

The Corfiote farmers are well aware of their indebtedness to the olive harvest and to the fact that in times of distress whole families have been sustained by the varied uses the tree provides. Preserved in brine and their own oil, olives have formed, with bread and goat's milk, the traditional food of the rural classes. When crushed the fruit gives oil which in its refined form is both a food and cooking medium of nutritive value. When the oil has been extracted the crushed seeds and pulp are dried and pressed and subsequently burned as a cheap if not pleasant-smelling fuel. The pulp is also returned to the land as a fertiliser or is mixed with winter fodder as a livestock food. The tree's foliage is often used as a bedding for sheep and goats and the wastewood provides fuel for heating and cooking or material for utensils and tools.

The services of the tree do not end with the varied products it produces. In the past the olive was suited to the confused political situation of the island when farmers were often forced to abandon their villages and fields. Under such circumstances a grainfield or vineyard left untended for any length of time would be ruined whereas olive groves suffered little damage.

Production-Methods and Marketing

Corfu is one of the principal olive-producing regions in Greece and its trees account for 48 per cent of the island's cultivated area and 50 per cent of agricultural production. In spite of its importance, however, the Corfiote methods of tending and harvesting are primitive and estimates reveal that with less time-consuming and wasteful methods the number of trees could be reduced by half without the yield being affected. Once planted out the tree receives little attention other than the periodic piling of earth around its roots to conserve moisture. Organic manure is infrequently used, weed control is insufficient and pest control inadequate. The chief destructive danger is the *Dacus* fly, and spraying trees with insecticide is essential. But many farmers are traditionally adverse to this practice, believing that killing insects causes an imbalance of nature. Pruning is also less evident than in other parts of Greece and the Corfiote groves consequently grow to considerable heights and develop extensive branches. Picking is now more common than in the past, but it is still general for the fruit to be left on the tree until it ripens and falls naturally to the ground. Large nets are placed to catch the fruit and to prevent its loss on steep slopes. By this method trees bear fruit every two years and in spite of a certain percentage of bruised olives the oil content is high. Picked olives are less ripe, produce less oil, and the trees have to be pruned to keep them small and manageable for the harvesters.

Although it appears that the Corfiote farmer does not lose by his primitive methods of gathering it should be stressed that the olive crop is irregular and lean years can be disastrous for the rural population. Much of the oil is consumed locally and in a poor season the effects are reflected throughout the economy in the reduced spending-power of many farmers. In view of the importance of the olive harvest laws are enforced by the Greek Department of Agriculture to regulate pruning and the cutting down of trees. These controls are major problems for the property speculators as trees can be owned independently of the land on which they grow and the owner has the right of way. Controls are also exercised in maintaining the purity of the oil and adulteration with vegetable oils is forbidden. Up to 5 degrees of acidity is acceptable – any more makes the oil strong and bitter.

All villages have their olive presses, many of which have changed little since antiquity. Jervis's description of a nineteenth-century press as 'a perpendicular stone wheel, revolving on a large horizontal stone of a circular form', holds true for the majority today, although the modern power-driven presses are increasing in importance and there are also modern collecting centres for oil refining. 'This press', Jervis continues, 'is set in motion by a horse, and bruises the olives which are shovelled in by a peasant. They are then placed in a mat bag, and pressed by means of a clumsy screw, the oil oozing through the bag into a hole cut in the ground: but the labour of turning the screw is so great that two men will not obtain more than 40–50 gallons of oil in one day.' The oil is collected into underground stone tanks to settle, and after a time it is considered pure enough to be sent to the bulk dealers. Following this extraction the waste material still contains a considerable percentage of oil which is used in the manufacture of soap for the local market. Every season the olive presses are blessed by the local priest who usually receives a quantity of oil in payment. The presses are worked by men and the olive collection is chiefly women's work – an excuse for gossip, laughter and singing in the fields.

THE VINE

The vine is one of Corfu's oldest crops and its cultivation can again be traced back into antiquity. But compared with the olive it is both time- and labour-consuming, demanding 160–200 working days a year. Over 17 per cent of the island's cultivated area is devoted to vines which generally occupy the more-favourable areas in terms of soil, slope and aspect. The fruit matures in August and September and consequently vines have to run the gauntlet of Corfu's dry summer months when the chief danger is shrivelling. To avert this risk the Corfiote vine is allowed to trail along the ground and only the grape-bearing shoots are supported by short forked sticks. The advantage of ground-trailing is that the plants present the greatest possible surface for the absorption of heavy morning dews. The low growth position also minimises exposure to summer heat and the thick foliage shades the soil around the roots. Side roots are often heavily pruned to induce deep growth of the tap root and, irrigation trenches are cut wherever possible to ensure an adequate supply of water.

The initial exportation of Corfiote grapes was fostered around 1880 by the French phylloxera crisis. Unfortunately for the island this was temporary, and today vines are cultivated chiefly for wine grapes which are used locally. Corfu produces an annual average of around 6,000 tons of wine grapes together with a small proportion of table grapes. The latter are usually grown in the warmest and best-protected locations. Corfiote white and red wines have good reputations throughout Greece but are seldom of consistent quality from year to year.

OTHER CROPS

Citrus crops also demand great care in cultivation and require special soil conditions and an adequate water-supply. Oranges, lemons and, to a lesser extent, mandarins flourish in sheltered valley and lowland locations particularly around Benitses, Potamos and Lefkimi. In recent years many new groves have been planted and the produce is used chiefly in the manufacture of local squashes and liqueurs. Corfu's unique liqueur is Koum-Kouat, produced from the fruit of the Japanese orange which flourishes on the island.

Apples and pears are the principal deciduous fruit crops and both are produced primarily for the Greek market. Other fruit trees include peaches, apricots, strawberries, cherries, figs and melons, and important nut crops are almonds, walnuts, chestnuts and carobs. The production of fresh fruit begins in April with the strawberry crop, followed by apricots, cherries and plums. These are followed by figs, peaches and early pears, and finally by maincrop apples. The consumption of fresh fruit has increased with effective refrigeration storage which extends the marketing season.

Grains play a less important role in Corfiote farming, the general position being that the islanders concentrate on the production of oil, grapes, fruit and vegetables and rely on imports to supplement cereal supplies. Collectively grains account for 12 per cent of the cultivated area with wheat, the chief crop, occupying only 3·27 per cent. Wheat and barley are grown under the system of dry-farming where land is left fallow in one year and cropped the following season. Patches of better and more moist soils, carrying grain crops, occur sporadically in small cultivated basins.

Corfu produces a wide variety of vegetables both for domestic consumption and for marketing on a commercial scale. Intensive vegetable production is concentrated around Corfu town and large quantities are sent to Athens. Vegetables fall into winter- and spring-grown varieties. Artichokes are important winter vegetables and tomatoes, onions, green beans, garlic and cucumbers are common spring crops. The production of potatoes meets domestic requirements and early potatoes reach the Greek mainland markets. Because of their high nutritive value broad beans and lentils also form a major part of the Corfiote diet. Small amounts of vegetables are grown for livestock fodder. Tobacco, peanuts, sunflowers and sugar-beet are grown on Corfu, but their acreages are insignificant.

LIVESTOCK

Within the last decade livestock farming in Corfu has developed considerably, chiefly in response to the tourist market. But it still remains backward and is primarily based on the raising of sheep, goats and unimproved breeds of cattle. Livestock have been traditionally kept to satisfy the requirements of the family in meat and milk, and animal products have rarely played a significant role in cash sales. One major deterrent to animal husbandry is poor-quality pastureland which although given as 23·5 per cent of the total area is inadequate for the purposes of modern pastoralism. As stated previously, the definition of pasture is a very wide one and generally refers to residual categories of land unfit for other farming purposes and with little natural herbage. On Corfu pastureland officially includes large areas of *maquis* upland with sparse thorny shrubs where only goats can feed, and even this is further deteriorating through over-grazing. At the same time orchards and olive groves are used for livestock – in fact all land that is not directly cultivated provides some sort of pasture, although generally it is of low quality.

The island's goat population has been variously estimated between 15,000 and 50,000. Omnivorous to a fault, goats do considerable damage to woodlands by feeding on the young shoots of shrubs and trees. The number of sheep is estimated as 65,000 and the unimproved breeds thrive on the short and wiry grass of the poorer pastures. Small improved flocks are found but these are generally kept close to the farmsteads. Often they are tethered to feed within olive groves and orchards or on small cultivated terraces after the crops have been harvested. Sheep and goats provide milk for cheese, wool for homespun cloth and blankets, and meat for important religious and family celebrations.

Corfu's cattle population is small but in recent years efforts have been made to encourage dairying. Most families own a cow which is usually tethered in a small area of improved pasture. The surplus milk sold to the dairies produces excellent butter, cheese and yoghurt. The island is also well supplied with poultry-meat and eggs. Village poultry production is on a small-scale farmyard basis with indigenous breeds of birds. Pigs are found in most villages and bee-keeping is common.

Horses, asses and mules are used for farmwork throughout the island, but the former are being increasingly replaced by tractors as mechanisation increases. Likewise the numbers of asses and mules are falling and their functions are being replaced by the scooter and scooter-lorry. Yet they still remain the beasts of burden of the Corfiote countryside and a major form of transport for the rural population.

INDUSTRY AND TRADE

Anstead's observation (1863) that 'the stranger looks in vain in Corfu for any special industry' is one not substantially altered today. The island's livelihood is dependent on agriculture and services, with tourism in the latter sector forming a major and increasing role in the employment structure. In comparison with most small Greek towns Corfu has its necessary and basic industries, but only 9·8 per cent of its active population are engaged in manufacturing. With its dependence on agriculture it is not surprising that food processing and beverages make up the largest branch, employing around 2,500 or 51·4 per cent of the manufacturing labour-force. The main products include olive oil, canned fruits and vegetables, preserves, juices and wines. Footwear, leather, textiles and clothing collectively form the next biggest group and account for 22·3 per cent of those working in manufacturing. Therefore, most Corfiote industries are small concerns, many being workshop establishments with a large proportion of one-man operated or family businesses. This is particularly true in the wood and furniture industries but it is also found in metal products (ornamental lamps, railings, doors etc), printing and paper industries. The fastest-growing industry is construction which is booming from the rapid annual increase in tourism. Cement, brick, breeze-block and tile industries are ubiquitous, especially in the environs of the town.

The trade of Corfu is similar to that of other Greek ports – the bulk of the imports coming from mainland Greece. The disproportion between exports and imports, which is a characteristic of Greek commerce, is well-marked in Corfu and the port derives its importance not from the bulk of its trade but from its commanding position at the entrance to the Adriatic. It thus services Greek, Italian and Yugoslav vessels plying between Italy, the Adriatic and the eastern Mediterranean – a marine function as old as Homer. In terms of passenger handling Corfu is second only to Piraeus and Patras, although this comparison is perhaps invalid for the former as the port of Athens and the country's chief industrial centre naturally attracts the greatest percentage of passenger and cargo traffic.

Corfu's old harbour lies between a detached breakwater mole

and the shore, but its depth is sufficient for small vessels only. It is the terminal for the Igoumenitsa passenger and car ferry. The modern port, with its expanded and extensive facilities, has ample accommodation for all vessels from small sailing yachts to the largest cargo ships and cruise liners. Here the scene is as animated as that found in any Greek-island port.

TOURISM

Corfu is a twentieth-century mecca for holidaymakers and the economic future of the island must rest to some considerable extent on its tourist trade. It still remains highly favoured by the British and rentable British-style villas have proliferated in recent years, as well as the number of hotels, many of which are of a particularly high standard. Most of the hotel accommodation is on the east coast but Palaeokastritsa, Glyfada and other western locations are rapidly developing as vacation resorts based on their scenic attractions and coastal amenities. The main concentration of hotel accommodation is in and around Corfu town where establishments range from those of extreme sophistication to small pensions which preserve their old-world charm. Holiday camps, youth hostels, camping sites, beach complexes and tourist pavilions are all on offer to the vacationer. Rooms for rent in private houses are common in the town but they are also increasing in the countryside especially at coastal resorts such as Benitses and Kassiopi.

A successful tourist industry is apt to bring with it tourist-fleecing, a falling off of traditional values and dignities and an interest in the foreigner for what he brings rather than for what he is. Fortunately such disastrous success has not yet reached Corfu but the future is unpredictable. The character of the islander is such that he recognises the value of tourism but as yet is not prepared to sacrifice personal dignity to the whims of the international jet-set. The latter arrive in their expensive yachts, for the island is a good stepping-stone between the western and eastern Mediterranean. The dockside provides facilities for refuelling, repairs and lengthy moorings. Palaeokastritsa also provides marine facilities and the Gounia area is being developed as a yacht marina.

Getting to Corfu provides few problems. The modern international airport is capable of handling most airliners. During summer it is busy with charter flights from most European

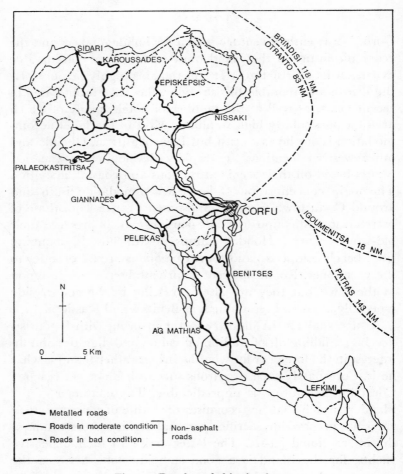

Fig 10   Roads and shipping lanes

capitals and it is also linked by regular daily flights to Athens. Pullman-coach services connect the island with the Greek capital via Ioannina and Arta. There are at least three buses a day and the journey, which uses the Igoumenitsa ferry to the mainland, is approximately 18 hours. The Greek State Railways reach Patras from Athens in 4–5 hours and the journey to Corfu is completed by ferry.

Italian and Greek cruise ships frequently call at Corfu and these are complemented by car ferries operated by Hellenic Mediterranean Lines in conjunction with the Italian Adriatic Line. This journey from the Italian ports is the most enjoyable and also the most economical method of travel for the visitor. On the new ferries from Brindisi to Patras, via Corfu, amenities and facilities are available to all passengers irrespective of class of accommodation.

For Britons interested in visiting or settling in Corfu the Britannia Club, founded in 1893, offers major benefits. The former ban on foreigners buying land has now been lifted but a government permit is necessary. John Forte's admirable guidebook discusses the problems and methods relating to settlement, land purchase and period of residence.

11   COUNTRYSIDE AND CAPITAL

CORFIOTE agriculture is conducted principally from a large number of compact nucleated villages varying in size from around 200 to over 2,000 inhabitants (Fig 11). These are connected by both rural tracks and surfaced roads and the main island villages are minor route centres. The density of rural settlement is high, but it varies considerably between districts and is chiefly determined by the availability of water-resources and productive soils. The north-east, dominated by Mount Pandocrator and its outliers, has few large villages, and only Episkepsis has a population of around 1,000 inhabitants. The barren broken slopes, however, provide meagre pasturage for flocks of sheep and goats and are relieved by erosion hollows with a richer soil base suitable for cultivation. These, together with the clay vales to the east where springs are more numerous, support a large number of small settlements.

To the west of Episkepsis and surrounding the main massif to the north are over 40 small nucleations, most with populations of under 500 inhabitants. The largest settlements are Karoussades, Avliotes and Magoulades. Here the Pliocene formations are retentive of water and the soils heavier and more fertile. Much of the north-west is closely settled, but villages are few on the alluvial plains. A string of villages occupy the northern slopes of the western extension of Pandocrator.

With the exception of a number of sizeable villages adjacent to Corfu town (Potamos, Alepou, Kanalia, Evropouli and Afra) and some small coastal settlements to the north (Gounia, Ipsos), the main centres of settlement in the north-centre of the

160

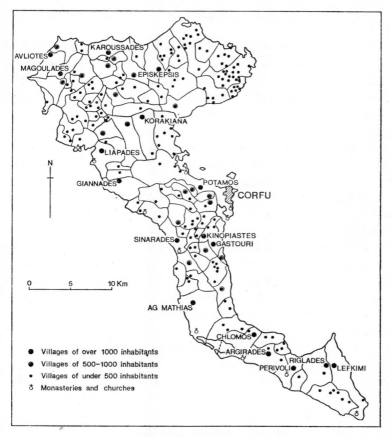

Fig 11   Villages and *kinotsis* boundaries

island are confined to the margins of the lowlands. The large villages of Liapades and Giannades occupy the eastern slopes of the western coastal range, overlooking the Ropa valley. To the immediate south of the town rural settlement is dense and a number of large villages (Sinarades, Kinopiastes and Gastouri) occupy the ravined slopes of Aghios Deka and its southerly extension. A string of settlements lie on the inner slopes of the Mesonghi basin, which although intensively farmed is itself largely devoid of villages. Aghios Mathias is the largest centre of this region.

In the extreme south rural settlement is chiefly confined to the spring lines along the slopes of the eastern hills, and to the low ridges overlooking the plain to the south-east. Chlomos, Argirades, Perivoli, Riglades and Lefkimi all have populations of over 1,000 inhabitants. Seen from the air this region has the appearance of a closely settled area where one village community merges with its neighbour. With the exception of a number of isolated churches the whole of the south-western coast is devoid of villages.

The names of the Corfiote villages are highly descriptive and a large proportion end with the suffix 'ades' as English place-names do with 'ton' and 'ham'. Other common endings are 'ani', 'ano', '(it)ika'. Some villages take their names from natural features, for example Potamos, near Corfu town, and Potami in the south-east (both literally meaning river). Other descriptive names are common but many have been corrupted by centuries of foreign influence and their exact meanings are lost. By far the largest group, however, are named after local saints (Aghios Mathias, Ag Dimitris, Ag Ioannis, Ag Theodori, Ag Markos, Ag Stefanos, Ag Athanassios, Ag Vassilos, Ag Spiridon etc) and as in most Greek islands there is a Profitis Ilias. Corfu also has villages that were originally paired for agricultural and land utilisation purposes and are recognised by the prefixes '(ep)ano' (upper) and 'kato' (lower). Examples, all within the Aghios Deka region, are Ano Pavliano and Kato Pavliano, and Garouna and Kato Garouna. Place-names like Palaeochori (old village) and Neochori (new village) indicate a population movement from the original settlement. The numerous isolated churches and monasteries, many sited on coastal promontories, naturally take the name of the saint to which they are dedicated – Ag Georgios, Ag Varvara, Ag Illiodoros, Panagia (Virgin Mary) Arkoudilos and Panagia Messavrissi.

Village settlements dominate the Corfiote rural scene but it is a fallacy to regard them as the only form of habitation. The isolated farmstead and the scattered collection of dwellings, which in the West would be termed a hamlet, are equally characteristic and today are proliferating as new land is reclaimed and families are breaking away from the traditional village existence. Modern road improvements and the decline of the economic, social and political motives for village life are the chief factors responsible for this development. Even so there are equally strong reasons for the continuation of the villages as traditional institutions and the farms and hamlets retain close links with their larger settlements and are governed by their local administration.

A variety of factors are responsible for the siting of the Corfiote village and for its high degree of nucleation. The preponderance of hillside or upland locations can be related in part to the security factor which in the past demanded that farmers should live in close groupings for protection. Rugged terrain offered some sort of defence in an island constantly subjected to invasion. Aghios Mathias, for example, is sited at 1,000ft on the western coastal hills, and Pelekas, above the Ropa valley, was sited in the seventeenth century to avoid Saracen raids. The comparative absence of true coastal settlements is testimony of the prevalence of piracy and raids from the sea, yet some do exist – for example Benitses a small fishing village sited on the shore – in spite of the dangers from the sea. The modern expansion of Benitses and other coastal hamlets such as Pyrgos and Ipsos is related to tourist development and their growth today is deceptive of their original functions. The inland villages maintained their own landing stages (*skalai*) which acted as small ports for craft engaged in fishing, transportation and local trade. Fishing practices have changed little over the centuries. It is undertaken from midnight until dawn –

now with the use of acetylene lamps. A traditional method is the use of a large net owned by a local syndicate. This is dragged out to sea each evening and pulled in the following morning. The catch has always been small in view of the effort required.

Water-supply has played another decisive role in settlement siting and is often the key to both the distribution pattern of communities and to their degree of nucleation. In general terms villages are located in areas where there is a supply of water and soils suitable for cultivation. Both factors, however, should not be over-emphasised for security was often the pre-requisite and it is still common for long journeys to be made from villages to streams or springs. This is perhaps best illustrated in the case of Corfu town where until the nineteenth century drinking-water was brought by pack animals from the Potamos river to the north. As stream courses are dry for a number of months they do not attract settlement and deep valleys are also avoided because of their tendency to develop temperature inversions during winter. Until recently the lowlands and alluvial plains were swampy and unhealthy and the persistence of malaria and other diseases favoured village locations at higher altitudes. The geological structure of the island also favours high-level springs, hence factors of defence, health and water-supply were often confined to a single location.

Two other factors help to explain village siting and the degree of nucleation. The first is related to the strong community spirit of the villager and the gregarious nature of the Greeks who are prepared to sacrifice economic advancement for the social advantages of living in a closely knit community. In view of farm fragmentation long journeys to and from often isolated plots and fields are more than compensated for by the sociability of group existence. The convenience of land exploitation is another factor. The shortage of farmland has dictated that villages are sited to permit the greatest use of agricultural possibilities. Village limits tend to incorporate a wide range of soil types and terrain, providing the community with areas of arable, pasture, rough-grazing and woodland. This is not always possible, but the *kinotsis* (see below) has been largely defined for this purpose.

VILLAGE MORPHOLOGY

Site factors are the chief determinants of the morphology and layout of the Corfiote village. Generalisations are difficult to make but settlements on hill-slopes are usually highly compacted with narrow tortuous lanes and alleys, and those that crown hill-tops, such as Varypades and Pelekas, often form an architectural pyramid of buildings, interrupted at intervals by church domes and belfrys. In less-rugged areas villages tend to be more spacious with gardens and orchards surrounding individual dwellings. On paths and roads leading to many villages a stone pillar with a recess for an icon, or sometimes a church, both guards and marks off the boundary of the community from the 'outside world'. On the outskirts too there is usually a cemetery with a small chapel beside it.

The ubiquitous feature of all villages is the *mesochori*, a central square, called in Corfu by the old name *foros* from the Latin forum. This is the focus of village life and around it are grouped a few cafés, the church and in larger centres, especially if the settlement is a *kinotsis* capital, the school and some unpretentious administrative building. The cafés serve as the main meeting-places for discussions and also function as tavernas and general stores carrying a limited range of produce. The family homes surround the square, but for privacy they are seldom aligned in regular rows and hence produce the irregular street pattern. Many dwellings have been subdivided in strict accordance with inheritance laws.

Living conditions show great variation between regions and many villages have been untouched by the island's tourist boom. Standards in basic sanitary and other facilities tend to deteriorate as the distance from Corfu town increases. This is a major cause of rural depopulation, both temporary and permanent. The responsibility for homes and farm buildings lies with the owners and cultivators and the general standards of comfort are unsatisfactory. The Agricultural Bank of Greece provides credit for improvements, especially to farm buildings, but a major modernisation problem exists.

Much of Corfu's traditional village architecture survives. The rural house is built of stone supplied chiefly from the Pandocrator quarries. Sinies in the north-east produces flagstones for pavements and doorsteps in both villages and town. In the south the local building stone is of poorer quality but supplies are available from Epirus. Brick is the main material for floors (storeys) and for the pillars which support exterior galleries. Roofs are tiled and are single or double-sloped, but not steep. Once constructed the houses are washed with brightly coloured rough-cast, frequently yellow or pale-pink, and the doors and window-frames are usually left white. The greatest decorative care is devoted to the village church whose coloured dome contrasts with the gleaming white of the main edifice and its belfry.

Although following basic plans, traditional village house types are rarely monotonous and a variety of architectural designs are employed (Fig 12). An original and characteristic feature is the external gallery supported by square pillars (A and B) throughout the length of the façade. The tiled roof is carried over this exterior. The style is also found in town houses but it is more a rural than an urban feature. The galleries provide protection from winter rains and summer heat and also serve as an open shed for a cart, agricultural implements and sometimes an olive press. These basic structures can easily be extended to provide a second storey (C). In the more pretentious dwellings (D and E) the upper storey is often reached by an external staircase and arcades and covered galleries make many villages look more prosperous than is the case.

Throughout Corfu, as in most parts of Greece, the traditional

Fig 12   Traditional rural house types

house types are being replaced by what can be termed 'sub-urban' styles – a change which indicates an increase in wealth but results in a drab uniformity of architectural design. These newer buildings of one or two storeys often appear incongruous and monotonous. The majority are built on concrete stilts with an external staircase leading to the living quarters. The rooms are constructed of hollow fired bricks and the house has an unfinished appearance. This is in fact the case, for additions can be made on top of the existing house (hence concrete supports are left protruding), to its side or in a good many cases actually underneath the dwelling. Until such time as the family ex-

167

pands or the daughters marry the space below is used as a covered yard for storage. This type of building is particularly common in the suburbs of Corfu town.

With the exception of the *demos* or urban district of Corfu town, the island is subdivided into just under 100 local and minor administrative units. These are generally based on the larger village settlements (Fig 11). Many are one-village units but others consist of a rural centre and a series of tributary settlements. The *kinotsis* is the lowest rung in Greece's highly centralised administrative structure of which Corfu is the capital of both the *nomos* and an *eparchy* of the Ionian Islands. A village with a primary school and a population of more than 500 (in practice often less) constitutes a local administrative community or *kinotsis*. This offers some measure of independent action in local affairs and a president and council are elected under the system of proportional representation. The president (*proedros*) acts as a combination of counsellor and chairman of local activities but his powers are limited for all major decisions have to be verified by the *nomarch* (prefect) of Corfu and often by Athens. The president is an unpaid official and is assisted in his duties by a secretary who is usually the local priest or schoolteacher.

Whereas the *kinotsis* provides neither full autonomy in village affairs nor a unified structure, it is called upon to maintain up-to-date statistics on population and village property and to prepare community tax rolls based on land tenure, produce and livestock. Land tenure in particular often provides major problems for the council, especially where its ownership is challenged and boundary lines are in dispute. The council formulates plans for the improvement of the village and its lands, but ultimately the decision rests with higher authorities.

CORFU TOWN

Corfu town is the only urban centre on the island and consequently it functions as a capital in every sense of the term. To the Corfiote it is referred to simply as the *poli* (city) and it forms the administrative, commercial, communication and social heart of the island. The town's present population of around 30,000 is equivalent to 30 per cent of the island's total, but during the summer months this figure is swollen by the influx of tourists. Population losses to other parts of Greece and emigration to Australia, South Africa, America and Europe is characteristic of the Ionian Islands and only on Corfu has the tourist boom begun to halt the flow. There is the added factor that whereas the dissatisfied in other parts of Greece move to Athens, the Corfiotes refuse to accept that metropolitan life is necessarily better.

The Townscape

Unlike most Greek provincial towns, Corfu was not affected by the destruction which resulted from the Greek War of Independence. Consequently the town has numerous buildings dating from the eighteenth and nineteenth centuries and it is this architectural continuity that contributes decisively to its character. It contains buildings related to each major phase of the island's development, up to and including the mushrooming growth of modern suburban expansion and tourist complexes.

Unfortunately considerable architectural damage was incurred in 1943 in the conflict between Italy and Germany and this was compounded by the Anglo-American bombardments of 1944. Large sections of the town, estimated as a quarter of the total area, were destroyed and many public buildings ruined including the Ionian Parliament House, the Ionian Academy, the Municipal Theatre and numerous churches. The bombing totally destroyed 525 buildings and those seriously damaged amounted to 320. Destruction of the old town exceeded 28 per cent of its total area. Open spaces in the heart of

169

the town still bear witness to the bombing, although extensive redevelopment has taken place. The main visual contrasts today are between the old town and its modern extensions which now engulf the suburb of San Rocco and merge with Garitsa and Anemomilos in the south and Mantouki in the west. The new town is built on a more regular and spacious plan and is characteristic of the vast majority of Greek provincial towns whose doubtful architectural taste and precarious harmony are the products of the late nineteenth and the twentieth centuries.

The south-western sector, centred on Theotoki Square and Alexandras Boulevard, was initially planned as a garden suburb. Its original principles of ornate villas and gardens have been largely replaced by the ubiquitous Greek apartment building and the Boulevard itself is largely devoted to garages and a motley array of small businesses sandwiched between more grandiose buildings. In comparison Garitsa, lying behind the British-built promenade, has successfully retained its village atmosphere as has Anemomilos, in spite of the proliferation of hotels and holiday villas.

The Old Town

Formerly confined within its fortifications the old town (Fig 13) has managed to preserve much of its original aspect with buildings dating from the Venetian, French and British periods. It is a palimpsest of the island's history and Jervis's description of its 'conglomerate appearance' remains true today. 'This town', states Forte, 'is Venice, Naples, a snatch of France and a dash of England, mellowed and mulled, like all good wines, until at last it achieves its own unique and in this case highly fascinating bouquet.' In few towns, and certainly in no other town in Greece, is it possible to step from an elegant French boulevard into a Neapolitan backstreet and emerge before some unmistakably British building or Greek church. It is this strange *rapprochement* of different architectural styles that makes the Corfiote townscape unique.

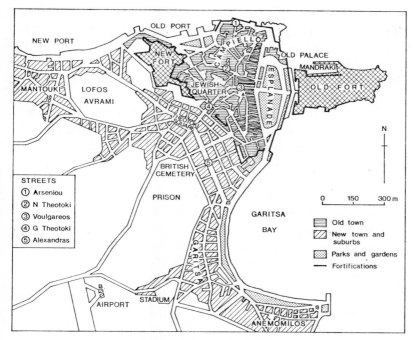

Fig 13   The modern town

The various stages in the development of the island were discussed in earlier chapters, although little was said how this was reflected in the town's morphology. Early maps and sketches depict the town contained within the walls of the old citadel. 'All the town', stated Pietro Casola in 1494, 'is built on a rock. They have good storage room for provisions and they collect water in large cisterns carved in the rock. The houses are numerous and so crammed that their roofs touch one another and the sun is not bothersome.' By the sixteenth century population expansion necessitated the relaxation of this strict defence consideration and a small undefended settlement developed outside the fortress gates. An open space, originally termed El Bazaro, separated the settlement from the citadel. This was later to develop into a garrison drill-ground.

171

Disaster awaited the unfortified settlement in the form of the Turkish siege of 1537 and awakened Venice to the necessity of constructing new defences, for provision of the citadel depended on the external marketing and handicraft quarters. Within a few decades a wall encircled the burnt-out ruins and a new fortress was built to the west of the walled precinct. The walls provided the security needed for urban expansion and reconstruction began in earnest towards the end of the sixteenth century. The area within the walls, however, was restricted and a large proportion of the 30 hectares (74 acres) was taken up by the Spianda (the parade-ground). Building restrictions produced a town that was compacted, with high narrow buildings separated by alleys. The Venetian governors limited the size of settlements outside the walls to avoid their use as shelters for invaders. Defence considerations also dictated the form of the town in the area of the Spianda where narrow streets leading off it at right-angles allowed cannon-fire from the old fort to penetrate the heart of the town. In times of siege this inevitably caused extensive casualties to both native population and invaders. The regularity of this part of the town was also related to social factors. The Venetians regulated the frontage area of residences so that their façades had no more than two windows. It is reported that this limitation was devised to reduce the number of 'privileged' ones.

The Campiello

The town's oldest and most picturesque quarter is the Campiello district. This is a maze of tall buildings, stepped streets (*skalinades*) and twisting alleys (*kantounia*) located between the old port, N. Theotoki Street and the Old Palace. Nineteenth-century travellers were struck by the irregular streets with their dark recesses and small enclosed squares. In Anstead's time (1863) the new town was rapidly expanding beyond its medieval confines and it was the visual contrast between the old and the new that fascinated him. The Campiello district was cramped and insanitary and its inhabitants were often subject to outbreaks of disease. Jervis, writing earlier, comments that 'the streets were nearly impassable from the offal of butcher's stalls, and the litter of the vendors of vegetables, who had been allowed to establish themselves promiscuously throughout the town'. The British introduced a series of sanitary regulations to clean up the streets, but few houses in Campiello possessed sanitary conveniences. Hence houses with WCs and adequate water-supplies earned the title 'English fashion' and charged high rents.

Jervis blamed the municipal council for the insanitary state of the old quarters. No alterations could be made to properties without permission, and this involved lengthy and complicated procedures.

> A request has to be made out, this is the work of the lawyer; the house has to be surveyed, that is the work of the architect; the owner of the house may be on bad terms with some influential municipal officer, and his request is consequently rejected. Besides, many people entertain a decided objection to submitting even the outward disposition of their houses to the scrutiny of a body of men, who in a small town like Corfu, make a subject of gossip for all their acquaintance.

Today the Campiello district, if still lacking in basic amenities, is a clean and picturesque quarter through which to wander and witness the form of an old Italianate townscape. Its tall tenement buildings (often six to eight storeys) tower above the narrow alleyways which are the hives of everyday local activity. This is the least-spoiled area of the town where washing hangs on poles over the streets. Fortunately cars are unable to penetrate much of the district.

Urban Architecture

In view of Corfu's varied history and rapid succession of rulers it is impossible to generalise on the town's urban architecture. Many Venetian buildings survive (ecclesiastical, municipal, military and residential) and a number have been restored. But the town's chief period of prosperity and building activity was the first half of the nineteenth century. Throughout Greece this marked the revival of neo-classical styles, especially for public buildings, although this revival is less evident in Corfu and the Ionian Islands where the traditions of earlier centuries were maintained. The Palace of St Michael and St George, with its austere Doric columns, is the island's major example of neo-classicism, although the Renaissance arcade of the Liston, which Young regards as a Palladian rather than a Greek revival, illustrates the more conservative ideals of nineteenth-century Corfu.

The present Town Hall is undoubtedly the best surviving example of Venetian public building. The fine sixteenth-century loggia was converted into a theatre in 1720 and until the early years of this century it was considered as a major European artistic centre for lyric and dramatic presentations. Following its destruction by air bombardment it was recon-structed on a slightly different plan and an upper floor was added giving the building its present appearance. The bust and relief on the external eastern wall represents the Doge Fran-cesco Morosini who defeated the Turks in the Peloponnesus (1684–7). Another Venetian reconstruction worthy of note is the now-famous Cavalieri Hotel at the southern end of the Esplanade. Formerly a dilapidated Venetian town house it has since been renovated to form a tastefully designed building which has preserved much of its original structure and character. Throughout the old town there are a number of Venetian colonnaded and proticoed residences.

The architecture of much of the town often appears earlier than is the case. Because of its restricted area the walled town was forced to grow upwards and owners who added extra storeys to the original low but solid buildings were obliged to continue in the original or a similar style. String-courses often, but not always, mark the level of earlier eaves which have subsequently been extended. The style that has persisted is an attractive one, but not always decorative, for the local stone is difficult to work. Arches and colonnades run down many of the town's principal streets and in the late eighteenth century the piers and arches were constructed of white Sinies limestone. Many of the gargoyle keystones, although eroded with age, are still in evidence. In the nineteenth century these were often made of plaster and brick like the house façades above them. Stone architraves, painted jalousies and tiled drip-courses jutting out over the windows are other decorative features. Moulded windows and doors are found but these are not all that common. Much of the domestic decoration relies on colour-washing where raised bands of white-painted stucco contrast with the ochre, mulberry, chartreuse and lemon of the main façades. Today the patchy whitewash, peeling stucco and seasoned wooden shutters speak of past grandeur. Tile is the ubiquitous roofing material.

Modern architecture is in evidence in the town, its suburbs, and in the countryside. Contemporary styles are chiefly associated with tourist development or with modern villas which are particularly ostentatious in the Kanoni area. The majority reflect neither Ionian nor Greek traditions and therefore are out of character with both their immediate urban and rural surroundings.

URBAN FUNCTIONS AND COMMUNICATIONS

Corfu is the marketing and commercial centre for the entire island and the pivot of its import and export trade. A large section of its population are shopkeepers and in characteristic Greek fashion fruit, vegetables, shoes and souvenirs clutter the pavements and streets. To a certain degree there is some areal segregation in the types of goods sold, that is streets or blocks are devoted to footwear, fish or meat products, fruit and vegetables and even WC and bathroom fittings! It is often difficult to distinguish retail establishments from artisan workshops employed in furniture-making and shoemaking or from the goldsmiths, silversmiths and tinsmiths. The rise in incomes associated with the tourist boom is reflected in the proliferation of gift and souvenir shops whose range of goods can be found all over Greece. Few souvenirs are made on Corfu and it is not uncommon to purchase a ceramic jug or plate manufactured in Stoke-on-Trent and hand-painted in Rhodes. The precise limits of the retail quarter are hard to define but its central thoroughfare is G. Theotoki Street which leads from the old town to Theotoki Square. Bisecting it are Voulgareous and N. Theotoki Streets and a maze of alleys devoted to retail and workshop activities. Much of the remainder of the population works in offices, hotels, travel bureaux and restaurants, and only a few are employed in small factories on the outskirts of the town.

Corfu town is the hub of a dense network of paved roads and tracks which link almost every rural settlement, if sometimes circuitously, with the capital. Many of the roads were built, extended or improved as part of the development plans of the various British High Commissioners. Many have fallen into disrepair and the majority are narrow and winding, but by Greek standards Corfu has an extensive network and one well-equipped with petrol and servicing stations.

For the tourist there are frequent local bus services to the main beauty spots, but elsewhere the island timetables operate to serve the needs of the villagers who arrive in town early in the morning and return late in the afternoon. Visitors who venture to the more isolated parts by local bus should be prepared to spend the night there. Theotoki or Sanrocco Square is the centre for buses serving the south of the island and has the air of a busy terminus. It is very much a working square and can be regarded as the main commercial pivot of the town. The terminus for northern villages is New Fort Square and the restricted suburban network operates from the junction of the two sections of the Esplanade. Visitors wishing to see the island quickly and cheaply can hire motorscooters and motorbikes, and bicycles for shorter journeys. The town has a plentiful supply of taxis and cars for hire.

For a town of its size, Corfu has a variety of clubs and

cultural institutions. The latter offer useful facilities for research into the history of the Ionian Islands. The archaeological museum houses most of the relics from ancient Corcyra and a Sino-Japanese collection is housed in the Palace of St Michael and St George. This was the gift of Grigorios Manos in 1919, the former Greek ambassador to Vienna. There are a number of historical archives, including one devoted to the poet Solomos, the Capodistrian archives which contain official documents relating to the 1797–1864 period and the Moustaxidi collection which are correspondences of the nineteenth-century Corfiote scholar with distinguished men of letters. They reveal much of the intellectual life and history of the island.

The Historical Archives of Corfu was founded in 1443 when a delegation was sent to Venice requesting that public documents relating to the island be placed under Corfiote administration. The archives have suffered great damage but they still contain valuable material on the town's administration, religious questions, trade tariffs and documents relating to health and sanitation. The Archives housed in the Old Palace, are efficiently catalogued and are freely accessible to research investigators. The public library also contains a rich collection of books, pamphlets and newspapers relating to the Ionian Islands in particular and Corfu in general. It houses a collection of reference books, historical novels and modern fiction presented by the British Council in 1966. The public library is complemented by the Reading Society which contains around 10,000 volumes.

Corfu is renowned for its bands. The Corfu Philharmonic was founded in 1840 to provide musical accompaniment to the St Spiridon processions. The intention was to replace British regimental music, but from the tone of their summer concerts it is obvious that the Philharmonic owes much to the 'brassy' sounds of the British militia. The band wears plumed helmets and the blue and crimson colours of the old Ionian State. It is composed of musicians of all ages.

...

LEISURE ACTIVITIES

Corfu town is no Palma, Lloret de Mar or Cannes. It caters
for tourists on a more sophisticated level and the night-clubs
and discotheques tend to be outside the town and part of the
holiday complexes and hotels. The average Corfiote's idea of
entertainment is a simple one and in many cases consists of
idly sipping a drink, spooning an ice-cream or a high calorific
cake at a pavement café. The café is an institution and a way
of life, acting as a meeting-place for discussion of items of local,
national and international importance. The Corfiotes, like all
Greeks, are avid newspaper readers and most European (and
American) newspapers, arriving the day after publication, are
available together with a plethora of newspapers and journals
which arrive from Athens.

The main social life of the town is centred around the French-
built Liston, the arcade of pavement cafés and patisseries overlooking the northern part of the Esplanade. In the past only
titled gentry were permitted to stroll and take their rest here,
but one can still witness the Corfiote counterparts of aspiring
'debutantes' and socialites sitting in small groups to see and be
seen. The Liston, with its shadowy lamp-hung arches, is the
ideal place to watch cricket. Tables are also extended to the
edge of the green.

The other main centre of social life, if less sophisticated, is
the area surrounding the old port whose large square goes
under a variety of names – George II, 10th Regiment and
Plateia Spilia. Here a few bars are open all night and are the
nearest equivalents to British and American bars. Although the
average Corfiote is not a big drinker of alcohol, the town has its
fair sale of ouzo, Greek cognac, resinated and unresinated
wines. Shops selling wines and spirits are nearly as common as
the souvenir shops and cater for the tourist market.

During the summer months much time is spent out of doors
and the evening *peripato* or *volta* is as traditional in Corfu as in
other Mediterranean towns. The main strolling ground is the

Esplanade, especially the southern section which houses the somewhat incongruous Victorian bandstand. Cinemagoing is an equally important pastime and a number of covered and open-air auditoriums attract large audiences irrespective of the often poor quality of the local Greek or subtitled foreign film.

Eating out, especially in summer, has always been a pleasure for the Greeks. There are a large number of restaurants, expensive by Greek standards, but also many cheap and more authentic backstreet establishments where there is sometimes music and dancing. Apart for a few specialities Corfiote food is much the same as that of the rest of Greece. *Souvlakia* (meat grilled on skewers), *moussaka* (baked aubergine and mincemeat pie), *dolmades* (vine or cabbage leaves stuffed with meat and rice), *domates yemistes* (tomatoes stuffed with meat and rice), lamb in various forms, simple and ornate salads, and a variety of sea-foods including octopus, squid, crawfish, whitebait and sea-urchins – although sounding different and tempting to the palate these can, after a few days, appear limited, repetitive and conservative in their preparation. The Corfiote specialities, therefore, are worth trying. *Sofrito* is a veal dish cooked in a rich-brown garlic sauce, *pastitso* is roast meat and macaroni in tomato sauce and *bourtheto* is fish cooked in red-pepper sauce. All meals can be accompanied by separate plates of vegetables, depending on the season, and a Greek restaurant meal is usually concluded with a fruit course – melon, watermelon, grapes, peaches, figs, strawberries or seedless oranges. The Greek fashion is to order a variety of dishes which are then shared by all.

Wines, local or imported from Greece, accompany a restaurant meal but for coffees (Turkish or instant), spirits and confections the *zakharoplasteion* (pastry-shop and café) is the place. Popular sweetmeats include *melomacarona* (honey cakes), *kurabiedes* (almond cakes), *mandolato* (honey and almond paste), *galataboureko* (custard covered filo pastry) and *baklava* (honey and nuts between layers of thin pastry). Corfu also produces a wide assortment of sweets including various crystallised fruits.

CORFU

For visitors, especially if they have indulged in a heavy oily meal the night before, Corfu offers a wide range of sporting facilities. Marine sports – swimming, skin-diving, water-skiing and sailing – are available at many localities. The town beach is at Mon Repos, but this is a poor replica of the sandy coves and wide stretches of safe bathing in easy distance of the town. There are clubs for tennis, football, squash, golf and horse-riding, most of which are open to non-members. The Corfiotes are also keen hunters and hare and woodcock abound in the thick scrub and olive groves. Wild duck is found in the Korisia and Antinioti lagoons, and snipe is common in the adjacent marshes and in the Ropa valley. The rough shooting season lasts from August to March and licences are issued by the police.

No visit to Corfu is complete without watching a local cricket match. An amusing account of the game is given by R. A. Roberts who arranged the international tour for autumn 1962 (*Playfair Cricket Monthly*). Although its popularity has somewhat declined, games are played every Sunday afternoon and sometimes Wednesdays during the season. The Byron and Gymnastikos clubs continue to organise visiting matches, a tradition which dates back to the annual visits of the Mediterranean fleet in the nineteenth century. Teams from Britain still compete in the cricket week organised in September, but the Corfiotes are happy to challenge visitors at any time of the year. Cricket terms are a corruption of Greek, English and Italian and it is not uncommon for ouzo to be ordered from the wicket or for an umpire to walk off the field in a Greek tantrum!

The very fact that cricket is played at all on Corfu is an anachronism. But this is part of the charm and character of the island. Corfu today enchants and delights, teases and, above all, tantalises.

BIBLIOGRAPHY

ANSTEAD, D. T. *The Ionian Islands in 1863* (1863)
ATKINSON, S. *An Artist in Corfu* (1911)
BAEYENS, J. *Les Français à Corfou* (Athens, 1970)
BAGALLY, J. W. *Ali Pasha and Great Britain* (Oxford, 1938)
BARRAS, J. *The Corfu Incident of 1923* (Princeton (NJ), 1965)
BOPPE, A. *L'Albanie et Napoléon, 1797–1814* (Paris, 1914)
BOWEN, G. F. *Ionian Islands under British Protection* (1851)
BRADDOCK, J. *Some Greek Islands* (1967)
BRADFORD, E. *The Companion Guide to the Greek Islands* (1964)
——. *The Mediterranean, Portrait of a Sea* (1971)
BUTLER, A. *Lives of the Saints* (1956)
CAMPBELL, J. and SHERRARD, P. *Modern Greece* (1969)
CHURCH, E. M. *Sir Richard Church in Italy and Greece* (Edinburgh, 1895)
DAKIN, D. *The Greek Struggle for Independence, 1821–1833* (Berkeley and Los Angeles, 1973)
DAVY, J. *Notes and Observations in the Ionian Islands and Malta* (1842)
DOUGLAS, D. C. *The Norman Achievement* (1969)
DURRELL, G. *Birds, Beasts and Relatives* (1969)
——. *My Family and Other Animals* (1974)
DURRELL, L. (ed). *Lear's Corfu* (Corfu, 1965)
——. *Prospero's Cell* (1970)
FORTE, J. *Corfu, Venus of the Isles* (Clacton, 1973)
——. *Wheeler on Corfu* (Clacton, 1972)
FOSS, A. *The Ionian Islands, Zakynthos to Corfu* (1969)
GEANAKOPLOS, D. J. *Greek Scholars in Venice* (Cambridge (Mass), 1962)
GOLDING, L. *Goodbye to Ithaca* (1955)
GOODISON, W. *A Historical and Topographical Essay upon the Islands of Corfu etc* (1822)
Greece (3 vols) (Admiralty Naval Intelligence Division, 1943)
HAMMOND, N. G. L. *Epirus: The Geography, the Ancient Remains, the History and the Topography of Epirus and Adjacent Areas* (Oxford, 1967)

HART, Sir B. L. (ed). *The Letters of Private Wheeler 1809–1828* (1952)
HASLIP, J. *The Lonely Empress: A Biography of Elizabeth of Austria* (1965)
HAZLITT, W. C. *The Venetian Republic 1421–1797* (1960)
HOLLAND, H. *Travels in the Ionian Islands, Albania etc* (1815)
HOMER (trans E. V. Rieu). *The Odyssey* (1946)
HOWARTH, D. *The Greek Adventure: Lord Byron and other Eccentrics in the War of Independence* (1976)
IRVING, C. *The Adriatic Islands and Corfu* (1971)
D'ISTRIA, COMTESSE D. 'Les Ioniennes' in *Revue des Deux-Mondes* (Paris, 1858)
JENKINS, R. *Dionysius Solomos* (Cambridge, 1940)
JERVIS, H. *History of the Island of Corfu* (1852)
——. *The Ionian Islands during the Present Century* (1863)
KARYDIS, G. P. *History of the Island of Corfu* (in Greek) (Athens, 1936)
KIRKWALL, VISCOUNT. *Four Years in the Ionian Islands* (1864)
KRACHT, T. *Korfu und das Achilleion* (Berlin, 1908)
LAWRENCE, A. W. *Greek Architecture* (1957)
LEAR, E. *Views in the Seven Ionian Islands* (1863)
LORD, W. F. *Sir Thomas Maitland* (1897)
MACKENDRICK, P. *The Greek Stones Speak* (1962)
MATTON, R. *Corfou* (Athens, 1960)
MILLER, W. *Essays on the Latin Orient* (Cambridge, 1921)
——. *The Latins in the Levant – a History of Frankish Greece 1204–1566* (Cambridge, 1906; reprinted 1964)
——. *The Ottoman Empire and its Successors, 1801–1827* (Cambridge, 1936)
MÜLLER, C. *Journey through Greece and the Ionian Islands* (1864)
MURRAY. *Handbook* (to Greece, 1840, 1854, 1872)
NAPIER, COL J. *The Colonies: Their Values Generally, of the Ionian Islands in Particular* (1833)
NAPIER, W. P. F. *Life and Opinions of Sir James Napier* (1857)
NICOL, D. M. *The Despotate of Epirus* (Oxford, 1973)
NORWICH, J. J. *The Normans in the South* (1967)
PAUTHIÉR, G. *Les Iles Ioniennes pendant L'Occupation Française et le Protectorat Anglais* (Paris, 1899)
PILLEMENT, G. *Unknown Greece* (1973)
POLITIS, J. N. *Corfou et les Isles Ioniennes* (Paris, 1864)
PROCOPIOU, A. G. *La Peinture Réligieuse dans les Isles Ioniennes pendant le 18 Siècle* (Paris, 1939)
REMÉRAND, G. *Ali de Tébélen, Pacha de Janina* (Paris, 1828)
REUMONT, A. *Sir Frederick Adam* (1855)

RODOCANACHI, E. *Bonaparte et les Isles Ioniennes* (Paris, 1899)
RUNCIMAN, S. *History of the Crusades* (Cambridge, 1951–4)
ST CLAIR, W. *That Greece Might Be Free* (Oxford, 1972)
SAVANT, J. 'Les Isles Ioniennes au temps de Napoléon' in *Revue Maritime* (February 1939)
SHELDON, P. *Greece* (1966)
SIMPSON, C. *Greece—The Unclouded Eye* (1968)
SITWELL, F. S. *Great Palaces* (1964)
THUCYDIDES (trans R. Warner). *The Peloponnesian War* (1954)
WILLIAMS, H. W. *Travels in Italy, Greece and the Ionian Islands* (Edinburgh, 1820)
WOODHOUSE, C. M. *The Greek War of Independence* (1952)
——. *The Story of Modern Greece* (1968)
YOUNG, M. *The Traveller's Guide to Corfu and other Ionian Islands* (1971)
ZIMMERN, A. *The Greek Commonwealth* (Oxford, 1911)

ACKNOWLEDGEMENTS

THE task of writing this book has been made very much easier by the help I have received from authors, ancient and modern, who have covered many aspects of the field before me. In this context I am particularly indebted to the writings of Lawrence and Gerald Durrell, Arthur Foss and Martin Young, who in their own individual styles have captured the atmosphere of the island and have greatly influenced my thoughts.

When writing the manuscript I was sustained by memories of the Corfiote landscape, the overwhelming friendliness and hospitality of the islanders, and the pleasure of sharing both in close friendship. I recall the gift of oranges from a peasant woman in Aghios Markos, the home-made wine of a Benitses taverna, a Sunday cricket match on the Esplanade, a veal and macaroni lunch at Ipsos and the view of Corfu town from the roof of the Cavalieri Hotel. These are a few personal memories of an island that gave me pleasure, contentment and an appreciation of the true values of life. I hope that I have captured something of the essence of Corfu in this book and that it will be taken as a token acknowledgement of the island's natural beauty and human warmth.

I also thank those who helped me in the preparation of this book. I am indebted to Mr M. M. Johnstone for the stimulus and companionship he provided during the book's initial research and for his advice and criticism on its content and style. My thanks to the secretarial, cartographic and photographic staffs of the Department of Geography, University of Strathclyde, Glasgow – in particular to Mrs L. M. MacIver who produced the maps and diagrams and to Mr B. J. Reeves who turned my photographic originals into presentable pictures. I am again indebted to Miss A. L. Laing and to Mrs J. C. Simpson for their assistance in typing the manuscript.

INDEX

187

INDEX

INDEX